G000255711

sum total

sum total

RAY GOSLING

POMONA

A POMONA BOOK P-005

Mad in England!

Published by Pomona 2004

1 3 5 7 9 8 6 4 2

First published by Faber and Faber 1962
Copyright © Ray Gosling 1962–2004

Ray Gosling has asserted his right under the Copyright, Designs
and Patents Act 1988 to be identified as author of this work.

All rights reserved. Without limiting the rights under copyright reserved above,
no part of this publication may be reproduced, stored in or introduced into a
retrieval system, or transmitted, in any form or by any means (electronic,
mechanical, photocopying, recording or otherwise) without the prior written
permission of both the copyright owner and the above publisher of this book.
Remember: don't get caught with your trousers down.

Pomona Books
PO Box 50, Hebden Bridge, West Yorkshire HX7 8WA, England, UK
Telephone: 01422 846900
www.pomonauk.com

Distributed in the UK by Turnaround Publisher Services Ltd,
Unit 3, Olympia Trading Estate, Coburg Road, London N22 6TZ

A CIP catalogue record for this book
is available from the British Library

ISBN 1-904590-05-5

Thank you: Richard Lysons
Original cover photograph by Roger Box

Set in 11 on 14.5pt Granjon
Typeset by Christian Brett

Printed and bound by Biddles, Kings Lynn

for

JOAN ELLIOTT

preface

I SIT HERE IN THIS BIG HOUSE. HOW BIG? DOES IT matter. It's big for my life, now: alone, rattled. A dried-out cold old pea in my house too big for me. Rattling? Creeping more like it. Creeping between piles of misshapen, scatological piles, and piles of the derititus of a long, long life: old wine bottles. Remember the label. Old scripts of things that were done — were they? Were they done? They *were* done. Made hundreds of Class One radio and telly. And campaigns for the freedom of this and the anarchy — ah — half-ripped newspaper cuttings of clippings that might have made a story I might have done. There's what I have done and what I might have done, all mixed together now. Oh, a piece I should have written, the research to nail that campaign further on that we/I nearly made a radio programme of, wanted to make that film, put forward that proposal that was rejected. Wasn't that what I did? Yes, ages of it. But the world has now turned I fear — fear? Ah just does and I'm not so wanted now. You got to be clever. You got to be slicker today than I am, was, ever can, ever could be. I see that now.

But that's why we were important, why this *Sum Total* is the story of a 'C' stream child. Not top material: not. Nor wanted to be. I was lucky to get away with what I did.

I'd written bits when I was 18, 19-years-old. Just sent them off and some got published/printed. It was how it was done then: *Peace News*, Colin Ward's *Anarchy*, *Tribune*, *New Left Review* and a pamphlet for the young Fabian Society. Then Faber and Faber wrote me a letter. Just out the blue — to me myself, 'Try at a book?' That was how it was: London publishing then. So we went up to town. There were meetings. Peter du Sautoy, Rosemary Goad, who became my editor. I was a poor boy, almost always been that. Poor old thing now — but then, as now, I needed to tap. Once on some smoggy afternoon (one forgets how the very air smelt then, of coal and choke — well, in some dim corridor at Faber's offices at 24 Russell Square) I shook the hand of ciggie smoking TS Eliot and very nearly tapped him up for a fiver/ten bob? A brown ten bob note. I didn't, as it happened. Too frightened? Aye. No, too respectful. One knew who was who: respect. Maybe I had been well enough educated already in grammar school. He was well dressed, Mr. Eliot, I remember. With thin lips and as tight, three-piece suited as a bank manager. People today don't know what a bank manager is. Am I right about him smoking cigarettes? It'll be in a notebook somewhere. Does it matter. I can't find it — my past is all here — ready for the bin: bin it.

There were parties at Faber's in those days and no one patronised me. No one was anything but lovely with me. I felt so proud and they were so good. One evening at a party, WH Auden, I filled his glass with red wine. Charles Montieth organised bits of advances and the book was done. And after it was out, well, we had good reviews. Richard Wollheim, Stuart Hall, Richard Hoggart, Francis Wyndham and lots of big folk said — 'Mmmm'.

Where would be the reviews? Kept and buried in this my now old man's mess. After *Sum Total* the world just opened up really for me. I strongly advise anyone to try their autobiography as early as possible. You'll never feel like that, like you did then, ever again. So I did all sorts of bits then for *The Times*, Nick Tomalin's *Town* etc., and then the BBC Home Service with Charles Parker out of Birmingham and then on my own and onto the Granada TV of Mike Scott. There were a lot of other things, building community groups. Oh lots, it doesn't matter.

Now I'm old. Old and this cold house: this house. My gardener, an old comrade, is going to call today with secateurs. We'll make a start.

I mean I'm going to chuck out, throw away piles and skips and bins of my life. Away, away, just chuck it. You can't keep. Too much in this world is kept. Life is for living and the weight of an archive/the nitty nuts and bolts drown/obscure with detail the spirit that was so this, this. No—all for the bin. I save this, this was my first book.

Sum Total was how my life began and it is full of the spirit of those early pioneer days. And I see now. The dreams of youth at the very beginning of the world—of the 1960s when it all began. I was there, beginning it with the first murmuring, almost incoherent muttering stumbling teenage fumblings towards what became the Great Rebellion that was to change the world as it had been. Because we said and acted out a NO that went on to change the world, we did. I did.

Our people did. Our generation did. This is how the ferment began in the heart and feet of white youth. There was only white youth then. That back then we/I said NO to family, past, church, religion, tradition, work as nine to five, as factory fodder; say no to the Lord and no to the Vicar and no to ownership. Yes, no to that for that enslaves and no, no, no, no, as to 'getting on', 'doing well'. Yes, we were against getting on — finding anarchic feet we wanted no control

Ah, this big house now. My old whole life is out of control. Wasn't that always what I wanted life to be — out of control for me. In the sense of not being reined in by the 'them'. Even success, especially success, be free; success enslaves you see, more than failures. Failures happen when you try. Success is addictive. It was free we wanted, to be as much as to do, free to my own control. To break from centuries of their control, to be free. Us to be free. That's what this book was to be: a youth's beginning. 'C' stream. I was not that clever and I wore that as a badge of courage for the world from now on was to shake, yes rattle and roll of course to the roars from the bottom drawers.

And now when I go out I look around me on the bus at, say, 8.25 of a weekday morning, and I'm bemused. Look at you. Having been freed by us, I look at you now and have you not with your inherited freedom, enslaved yourselves. With your focus ladders, mobiles and your text-phones. Trapped yourselves into private circuits of self-enslavement just like rich people living on gated estates have enslaved, imprisoned themselves. When we wanted the freedom of the whole wide world. Speak to strangers. Yes, yes, yes. Smile at the day. Not that now I go 'out' much, not now. Not lost your marbles? No, nah, just a rattling old crust: crumb more like, withering in this big old house stacked high, every room near enough now with stuff half sorted. I'm imprisoning, entwining myself. Maybe we all do. The gardener is coming.

But you, you I see from the top of the bus, for I do go out more than I admit when I'm grumpy. I do go out. I do look about me as I always did. I do see — and you scurry without the time to stop to stand and stare. Oh: sorry for you, I look down on you from the upper deck on the bus — so you're into 'your thing'. Into your thing. Which is often some thing 'they' have sold you. You have 'willingly' let yourself buy what is marketed for you to think it is yours and it isn't, my dear. We set fashion. It was later that fashion and marketing caught on to our rebellion to sell a rebel-look that's newly enslaved because you have to buy it. The punter has to buy the merchandise. We didn't buy. We created. We were never punters and never followed.

New Establishment. Fall into line — be qualified? Do as you're told. Jesus, no more school we cried. I hated University. My two terms of it described in this book. Just horrid places. Be focused? We wanted blinkers off — hello. In our naivety we wanted, I wanted, to speak to strangers, consider the chaffinch in the hedgerow, the ripple on the river, the sky at sunset. Wanted to hold hands with the world and I did and more than hands.

So when I see texting on the mobiles — into their own circle? No, no come on: don't. We wanted to break the circles, step off ladders, walk proud outside the squares, sing freedom.

Oh it was lovely to be young as I was and, in 1959, when this book was begun, inspired by the early rock 'n' roll

You're the future. I just go back. I'll not skip this book: a piece of social history I'll keep this to hand on to you. How we wanted freedom and won it. Wangled it, wrung it out of a world as it was then—ours, oh how fixed, how straight lined. You could see the old ways, then. See and smell work, church, do as your father says. See the masses regulation Montague Burton suited up in their congregations at factory gate and church fête, on their knees, and with hands up sometimes for a socialism, that old LS Lowry working class England we wanted no part of and yet in this *Sum Total* I'm surprised I tendered respect for.

I had respect for my Dad. He was self-made. Not made to make money or made to get on. But made to make himself a life that suited his idea of a life and style he could live with at ease. I was so lucky. And my Mum, she loved the flyness in me. Yet though we were the very, very first teen age we never foul mouthed, rotten rubbished the old. We had respect, manners you know, towards the old. It was just we were not going to be part of it—for more and deeper reasons than just as it had been, has been. Do as your father says. We wanted a new, new world. Our world. We were vague about that, in its particulars. But we got it, in its spirit it came to pass. By us.

And I—I did: did it—and this fumbling beginning, *Sum Total*, was my foundation for a life of doing my bit at opening eyes and keeping cheer and clear and openness. That's what I went on to do in the documentaries I made for 35 years. I was in the fields, so to speak, of the little things of life. Half-hour programmes to praise The Allotment, Sheds, and another half-hour—The Caravan. Portraits of places. Not London, Paris and Rome, but Goole, Weymouth. The little things of life are more important than the big things.

Ah, where's the gardener? How much can I load in one afternoon into one skip? My end turn—there we are. It's your turn now. Oh, look at the adverts saying do it, do it, do it. And don't do it. You're bigger than that.

Man is the weakest 'C' streamer. Don't fall for what they sell you. Be open and take of the free things — the air — and make your life your own good way

Mine? My Sum Total? Just lovely: lucky boy. Well lots of us were.

You can too.

Ray Gosling
August 2004

one

I READ THE PAPER. STANDING OVER THE MARBLE-topped bar I read the paper. Says I'm tired, played out; that I've shocked parents, stirred nationwide publicity, and that I have left this city. This paper, it tells me I'm on an extended holiday with friends in the North. Int that nice — bloody lie. I'm here, still in this city; waiting for a train to take me south. At last I'm going away. I don't know where. I bought a ticket for London, but I don't know. I fancy going home for a start. Whisky — feel it burn all the way down. Cigarette — feel the nicotine cling. That woman in green, she needs some lessons in how to pour beer. The bloody trains they're late again. Not surprising, everywhere there's fog. I love You. I love You. Write it with the wet beer on the marble. I love You. That's why it's taken so long for me to get out of this place. When Leicester went bust, there was only You to keep me here. But now I've got to go. I can't stay any longer. But I tell you this: when all this is over I'll be back. Don't you worry I'm coming back; back to Banners and The Ratcliffe, Le Gourmet and The Marquis and The Old Barley Mow, and all them places I can't really name. I have, I do, I love You.

I have got to get away. My only luggage, my only tie, my only connection, only thing I have left from this place is You. And now if I go away all I'll have will be a picture, a memory; a ghost walking into my tiredness as I wait for trains, for a lift by the roadside. That feeling that eats at my guts as the train rocks across some switch, some anonymous set of points. It'll be a memory calling up to me from the record bars and radio shops as I wait high up in a truck's cab to get through Doncaster on a Friday at five. It'll be a dream of footsteps in the hall, the turn of a key in a door; the name of this city, of this part of England; the voice of Nat King Cole on Cable Street. Another whisky. I want You. I still want You. I want to get rid of all the tears and sweat and blood and the laughs of this place. I want to cry it all out of my system, get it all on one record in an old beer cellar; an afternoon, a whisky bottle and running fire; everything fun and over-flowing and too rich; and the volume turned up so the sound don't mean a thing anymore.

I'm waiting for this train; and all the time I keep thinking about You, and I'm clogged up, and the whisky burns slowly down, and the cigarette smoke gets forced down through where the drivel and statements and lies have come from, right through to where I know I love You.

If I lean back my head, just one little bit, I start spinning all around inside. I feel sick, right up to the eyeballs; sick of a music that's taken me down and down and down; and I still love You. I want to draw back your hair to where it meets the skin, and feel your blood pumping on and on behind your closed eyelids. I got that feeling that all this has happened before, but I know it hasn't. This is the first time I've ever felt so full and sick right through. One day You'll read this, and by then it'll all be over and we'll both have got over this and we'll both have moved along and apart; but when You read it You'll say just as You always said: 'I know. I know.'

Are you with me? I know there's room for improvement. All the words and all the pictures just won't be able to get across what I feel like leaving this place behind. I loved this place, just as I loved You. But now it's all bust up. Things'll never be the same. All the gossip and the talk, it's found its semi-colon. From now on my only penetration will be my moving around. There is blood on my lip where the paper of the cigarette has torn at the dried-up skin. I look into the whisky and try to think. Think. Think. What have I got from twenty-one years? What made me go into this place? Why am I getting out? Where am I? What have I got for these twenty-one years?

I love You, but the show's over. The show in this place is finished, and I've got to move on. If anyone should ever ask You why I left; why I had to go, tell them I left because of You. If it hadn't been for You I would have fought through and carried on. But it wasn't like that. You were really there.

I'm waiting, waiting for this bloody train. Why's it take so long? I look at my face in the mirror behind the Vodka bottle. I got a black eye, a real and very rich black eye. I start on the questions again. Why has all this happened? Who am I? Do I really know? Aye for sure, I can read my name in this paper, and it isn't all lies. It says quite a bit about me. It int all lies. No, that won't do.

Try again. I am one of the little people, anonymous, and I'm going away; and wherever I go I'll still be the same wild and rather frightened little man. I'm not scared of anybody.

I'm just scared of myself. I'm like a traveller. I shed a skin at this place, leave my little message — Kilroy was here — and move on to another red blot on the map. I take away a memory. Get rid of a skin. Then I move on.

See that Strand Ad: lonely young man, trilby, raincoat, in the middle of the night, any street, any city — that's me. Like a bug, like some creepy crawly thing moving across all them maps in an atlas, looking and listening and making notes in a small black book like a man from MI6. One of the rootless, self-made refugees, and I have to keep moving for fear I might discover myself — to be nothing; for fear that some student might slap me on the back and break into a private dream; for fear I might become involved, have to take sides, get committed; like a Mr. X from a Graham Greene entertainment — one of the little people.

Standing at bus queues, on railway platforms, airport lounges, on quaysides, at coach stops never feeling quite at home. Coming from and going to but never arriving, never departing, always passing through. Seedy, unpresentable, holding the tipped cigarette as if it were love like the singer holds the hand mike, and then drawing on it like it contained some secret quality, everlasting life or death, or complete immunity. I walk back and forward, hands deep down in my pockets, feeling my money and secretly counting it like a miser, and then as if regretting my care, as if I didn't want to have all this unclean dirty loot, as if I didn't want to be weighted down any more by this medieval coinage, spending it on bars of chocolate I don't really want, drinks that won't mix, cigarettes of peculiar brands, without any reason or purpose but just to get rid of the stuff, take all the weight out of my pockets. I'm one of the little people as creeps on you, tries to crawl right inside of you; one of the refugees who should have been left behind, or got fitted in on a shelf, or found their place somewhere in the pattern of things.

I'm a little one-eyed flea. I and my savage eye — no, none of this, not really. I arrived only because I had to stop to get petrol. I'd run out of cigarettes. I stopped, and I found I liked it, and so I stayed. Simple.

But then after I'd been here a bit I thought I knew. I thought I'd found the place where I belonged, the job I liked but I didn't; I hadn't. And so now; now all this is over. Now I've got to leave I want to push across, retch on retch all the shapes I can remember that seem to make up the puzzle — why I turned up in this place, and stayed, and now why I have got to go.

Why am I here? What am I like? And where do I go from here, after I've come through? I want to find out, and to do so I want to go back, back to the things that brought me to this place.

The train comes in. I get on it. The churnings of this tired out mind keep on. Look to your family, your home, where you came from. You were promised a future as wide as Texas, the chances your parents never had. You threw the dirt on yourself. You did yourself down. There's no hard feelings. It just turned out this way. At the back of you is the greatest phoney of them all, the biggest cheat of the lot of them. You couldn't stick anything long enough to reap in the goods. You've seen a great deal, but you don't know a thing.

No, no, no. I have seen the tired suits of the crowd. I have heard the diary read aloud. I have seen the love letter passed to the Judge. I have read the telegram that stopped the clocks. I have dialled for the time and heard at the third stroke. I have been sick on the crossing to Calais. I have felt in my pockets and found the black king of a chess set, with the cross on the top. I have felt the spot where the hair meets the skin. I have fallen in love with the wrong person at the wrong time.

And now I stand in the corridor looking back at the platform — theme music — and when they write the book of the film they will preface it with 'De Profundis'. Looking back at the platform as the train pulls through the tunnel, looking back as if You were there, as if You were waving good-bye from the platform. You are.

The fugitive kind will follow their kind. I was too involved. I made mistakes. The witchhunt: it's over. Only my own questioning voice is left. I take a seat, and look out of the window.

two

A CEMETERY. FOG. THE SODIUM LIGHTS ON THE DUAL carriageway shining red through the waves of mist before the darkness comes down and they change to orange. It doesn't matter now. The trains are bound to come through. It doesn't matter in any case. In the fog. Ninety-seven miles from London. Three miles from You and all of you. Going away. It doesn't matter at all. I have seen my name in the University news-sheets. I have seen my name on the news-boards in blue pencil. I have seen myself quoted in the posh magazines, the essays, the references, and the letters to the editor. They talk of me over coffee every now and then. They point as I walk across the rubberised floor. I am going away. We pass a deserted station, You and I. The trees have a dirty snow cover where they meet the ground. A little girl plays with her starlet cosmetic kit. A women in black cap and coat, with white hair, smiles at the child. I smile at You. There's a river. We cross. It is growing dark. I am too tired to wipe the sweat from the window pane. The other passengers are not interested. We are all alone. The falling day's ball of sun looks like an electric filament and shines through the tracks of perspiration on the window. It is cold outside. The land is blurring. It is blotched by the grey snow on the black grass. Another station. A small freight yard. I shall lean over and my head will touch Your shoulder. A signal box. A stream. I have taken a non-smoker. I want a cigarette, but I shall do without. I want to kiss You, but You aren't there. Even that doesn't matter. Nothing matters any more, at all. The woman has dropped her head and dozes. Her legs are fat and her bootees are fur-lined. I want to put my hands around her neck and close her existence, but I won't. I shall not smoke in a non-smoker. I shall sit still, and wish I had taken a smoker. I want You. I am going into the corridor to smoke a cigarette. I look at You who are not there. A cottage. The train rocks. I shall sit still. I must have a cigarette. I think, and I do not think I think. I cast my mind back to a bar, and a return I know I shall not make, to a bar where You wait, where I could have taken another whisky and forgot; the name on the notice-board in the student's scribble, the name in the press, the stares of strangers, the bitterness in others, the remarks of an acquaintance, the laugh behind a door, the knowing smutty smile. There is more on earth. I shall forget. Bitterness will be my own regret. Memories will merge in time. The train has stopped. I get up, and tread over the legs, and out of the door. I still have to smoke that cigarette.

Again I am waiting on a railway station. Waiting for a connection. I shall go home again. Home? No: to that town where I was born; that town where my parents still live and work. I make my connection, my first connection; my first move, across on a branch line to where I unwillingly came into this world. It is dark and the train is dark, and my compartment is dark. I have a smoker, but I still have to light the cigarette. The chuffs of the steam engine echo across the valley. On the other side from where I sit there is a man with a scar where his moustache should have grown. Alongside sits a boy of about nineteen wearing jeans smeared with the dirt of the earth. His face is red and there is a country flavour with him. His shoes are black, clean and toe-capped. He is reading a weekend magazine. The man is reading *The Listener*. I am making notes in a little black book.

Somehow You do not fit in on this railway line that joins two major arteries of communication. I feel I left You behind on the fast train south.

We have stopped at a station where the lamps are lit by oil. No one gets in. No one gets out. There are no connections to wait for The train bounces. It does not rock like an express, like the train I left behind.

You belong to that fast, that big beat, that gas trunk from London to Manchester; the boat train from Liverpool; the Scotch express at York; the two stops Bradford, Leeds, Saint Pancras; the Irish Mail at Crewe.

I have also been more at home, more at peace with myself in that; yet I don't feel uncomfortable on this branch line. The man is chewing his hand. To the left, above the vacant centre seat at my side is a mirror; and opposite that is a print— Penrhyn Castle, near Bangor, North Wales—runs the legend. We have stopped again. The man with the scar is reading *Robbespierre the Incorruptible*. The boy is reading *I'm afraid I'll betray my husband*. The man is very agitated. He wears thick knitted socks and brown trousers. He keeps crossing and uncrossing his legs. That man, he must be wearing a short-sleeved shirt.

Nowhere to go, and nothing to do, all I can think of is that I was in love with You.

The boy turns two pages, a third, folds the paper and reads. I mustn't look at them any more, or they may look up, and I may lose my little black book. The terrible thing about having a bad memory is that you have to put down on paper observations, thoughts; it's all so time-consuming. I scratch my head with my fingernail, and I sniffle. I pick a piece of cotton from my trousers, very carefully. I must not offend public decency. I scratch my leg. I bite my nicotine nail. The roof of the compartment is plain. Soon I shall have forgotten the talk and gossip of a hundred bystanders and observers, and shall be a nobody again. The jokes, the face of the too-important person who refuses to acknowledge the passing of the time of day. The official who asks for a loan. The London-bound express I left behind will be going through Wellingborough now. Our train stops at another wayside station. The porter shouts the name and we move again, across a road where a line of cars with yellow headlights wait for the gates to open. I shall be glad to get home, home. No, I shall be glad to reach another point. I am glad to be on the move again. I am glad I'm away at last from the intrigue of people for positions that don't exist anymore.

Why did I change trains? I took a ticket for London. I don't want to go on. I want to go back; not to all that but to You. I want to go back to that train and You, and take You on to a little place I got in Camden Town. It's too late. I'm already one move away.

The boy is reading *I'm not ready to marry yet — Elvis*. The man is reading a poem called *The Yellow Girl*. We have stopped again. I was invited to spend a month in the summer at a little village in Suffolk, a nice family but I don't think I shall go. I don't care. It doesn't matter. Next week I shall be back in Paris. Maybe.

One day I shall be dead. It doesn't matter. But here I am, now, on a branch line stopping at every station on the way to the town where I was born. I don't know why I didn't stay on the other train. It can't be much above fifty miles from London now.

I do not think You were ever in love with me, but that doesn't matter. It is sufficient that I should want You, and it was sufficient that I loved You. You may have had a certain liking, even a certain affection for me; but it was money and pride more than love. It doesn't matter.

I think I look good tonight. I feel annoyed that no one but this man who twitches and this boy of the earth should see me like this. I should like You to see me. I have had a shave and a wash. I'm wearing a new white shirt with gold cuff-links. My nose needs blowing. My shoes are new, Italian with good suède uppers, and pointed toes. I think that if I blow my nose it'll bleed. I can feel a trickle of blood right on the bridge. I had my hair cut and razored, and all done up this morning. That man is picking his nose with his fingers, and he thinks I can't see him behind *The Listener*, but I can. He's crossed his right leg over his left. The boy has put his paper in his pocket, and looks out of the window. I look at my watch. We must be nearly there. A man with a suitcase is passing in the corridor. I leave the compartment, and go out into the corridor, and I light a cigarette, and stand by the open window and look out at the lights of the town I was born in. The cold air, it should stop my nose bleeding any further. It doesn't matter. The freight yards, the goods depot and we're there. I am — home. The train stops. I open the door, walk along the platform. I explain to the ticket-collector why I am on the wrong train, and I pay the excess, walk through the booking hall and up to the taxis. I turn back and take a taxi into the centre. I pay the driver off but I don't tip him. I stand in the centre of the town, the place I was born in, stamped on my passport with the colour of my eyes. Being born here is an unescapable fact. Like the colour of my eyes, there's nothing I can do about it. There is drizzle and dirt. I hear the local people talk in the local way. I do not like it here, and yet I'm as much a native as they are. I should be speaking and working and living like them, but I'm not. Some of them look at me as if I was a stranger from another planet or something. I want to shout at them. I was born here. My family lives here. I too am of this people. This town is my town. The facts, they're true; but they don't fit any more. The emotional skins that once held the facts have been shed long ago, gladly thrown away. No use for them any more. I don't belong. Don't want to come back to this town as 'my home'. I have left here. I went away a long time ago. I have only come back to ask you a question, a simple question. What you got to tell us, our town? I int going home. I'll stay to have a beer, and then I'm on the road again. Come on, I'm not going to be here for more than an hour or two. Come on, what you got to tell me? You must have something to say. I was born here. I come back to see you, because I'm passing through. I wouldn't pass so close without calling in to see what you got to tell me. But I'm not going to wait for ever. I have to move on. Tell us our town, what you think about us now? Been a long while. Tell us, our town. Tell us.

three

SO YOU GOING TO TELL US? YOU WERE BORN HERE. YOU were brought up here. We gave you the money to go to a University. This is your home.

Is it? I feel no sense of belonging. It's just another town to me. Someone may recognise me if I walk down Bridge Street, but that isn't unusual. It applies to many places. The chances are just as even in more than a score of towns. I have no sense of being home. I was born here. I went to school here. I have friends here. I have been happy here. I've been very unhappy too. These are just facts that I tag on the end of the name as I see it on a map — Northampton: and I tag those things on the end. Just as I can do for a score of cities and towns. I cannot say truthfully — I come from Northampton. I feel no sense of being an old Northamptonian. I was born here, and brought up to some extent here, but that is all. I cannot say for you what I can for Liverpool or Nottingham: I have liked it here. I have never worked in your town. I have never lived on my own in your town. There is nothing to hold me here. My parents live here. That is all.

We have not disowned you, our kid. You've disappointed us very much, but we haven't disowned you. We know how you must feel just now. Come back. We shall not mention our disappointments. We won't drag up the past. Come back.

Be sensible. Settle down in your town, at least for a while, till you've sorted things out.

No, I shall have gone away before morning. But let me start at the beginning, and tell you; try to explain why I'm not coming back. Walk with me down to the river past the new American cosmetic factory I haven't seen, but have heard so much about in your letters. Walk with me down to the river and I shall try to explain. I wouldn't like you to get the wrong idea. I have many memories of this place. This is where I grew up. Let me start at the beginning.

My mother was a school teacher. Her parents were farm workers on an estate in Cambridgeshire. She taught at the local C of E school in the village, and then moved on to council schools in Sussex, Dagenham, and Huntingdon. She was an infant teacher., and from what I've heard she was a good one. All I know is that she was very conscientious. I see her as a small, sensitive and wonderful woman, with the fields and farms of that part of Cambridgeshire still very much a part of her; a wonderful mother. We've had the ups; we've had the downs and we've come through fairly evens.

On her side of the family there was my grandad. I remember the time he came to see us at our semi-detached house just after the war, standing in the back garden by the rockery looking bewildered and all lost and out of place. I've got a photo of him somewhere, with his pipe and his hands straight down at his sides, standing bolt upright and looking straight into the camera, with the back garden behind. I remember as a child going out to stay with them in that little village, in a little white cottage by the green where the lavatories didn't flush like ours at home, but there was a bucket underneath which smelt and had to be emptied twice a day. I liked it there. Every time I went over I felt very happy, and free, and I think it did me a great deal of good going away from the town and changing buses at Bedford and St. Neots to that sweet and stiff unspoilt village, with its three chestnut trees on the green.

There was always the smell of cooking. I have never smelt anything like it since. Perhaps it was bread or the meat on the spit. Perhaps it was neither, but whatever it was there was this wonderful strong and tasty smell of cooking constantly coming from an open stove above the fire and the black enormous kettle that was like the cooking, always hot and steaming. There was watching an Uncle feed the pigs, and the first time I ever saw piglets. They were rolling in the mud around a big black sow; and there were hens and chickens. I was frightened of them chickens. And the whole idea of the country was strange and frightening and uncivilised and wonderfully fascinating. I always seemed to be happy out there, whether it was just for the day or for longer. Never been able to recapture this early excitement with the country. Now green fields are just a view from a window, to be got past as quickly as possible. But then I would love to walk across the ground with my grandad, over the estate and up to the woodland, and along by the fields of corn; grandad with his moustache and his pipe and shooting pheasants. I can remember watching from the gates as the men were harvesting and shooting the rabbits as each bit was finished. I can remember going for a walk at what seemed to me then to be a very late time to be up and out, and going into a field and seeing hundreds of rabbits, and they didn't run away, and someone told me how destructive they were, and showed me why and I could understand why I mustn't be sentimental over these rabbits. I can remember then asking why someone didn't shoot them, now, and being told that it was because they hadn't brought a gun. I was always, both at school and before and even now asking those silly questions, like that; questions that had obvious answers if only one thought for just a second, but I always and still do come out with these silly questions. I am never quite sure that there might not be an obscure, or another reason or answer. I want to be told that what I thought but didn't say is right; and so out I come quite unconsciously with the silly question, to confirm my own unspoken answer.

But most of all on my mother's side I remember Uncle Will, mother's brother. He wasn't married, and never said anything. Lives all alone and has a housekeeper in, and he's gardener up at the Lord's estate, working at the Hall. I have always liked Will; a great admiration for him, his sameness and the life he leads. I don't suppose he'd know me now, and I wouldn't be able to recognise him if I passed him in the street; but as a kid I can remember watching him and wondering what it was like to be all alone in the corner, all silent and alone, and having the same job all these years in what seemed to me feudal conditions. And then there were the relations who kept the pub, and walking with Aunt Sis with her sing-song voice down in the cellars at the pub, and they let me taste the cider but not the beer. And there was great, great Aunt Lizzie who sat in a rocking chair in a garden of rambling roses, and was all white hair and black shawl. She reminded me of a raven, ready to croak and bite and pounce and do all the bad black things that ravens must do, and yet she was always so wonderfully sweet to me. And there was the uncle who was half blown to bits in the First World War, shouting and grunting meaningless sounds as he loaded hay on to a truck, and then limping across and shaking my hand and screaming and laughing and I was very frightened and people said it was a shame, and that he was very intelligent, and couldn't help it, and how it wasn't his fault, and he was lucky to be alive. And I thought alive; that is being alive. I can remember a pond that seemed like death because it was deep and still and I was told not to go near it, and geese would cross the road above the pond. And then one came to the green and the post office and the little white house where an aunt who made jam lived, and the miles and miles of flat land. There was a church with a steeple, and a few council houses on the main road. It is all very vague now, just a blur and a memory of a place where it was all quiet and flat and where I was very young, and everyone loved me, and I was frightened and fascinated and very happy. It's a memory of the smell of cooking, of beer and Uncle Will sitting in his corner smoking his pipe. A memory, vague, blurred.

Every Christmas my mother would bake a special Christmas cake for Will, and we'd send it off by registered post, and he'd take months to reply, and we'd all wonder if he was alright, or if the cake got there, and then when the reply did come it was a short note in black almost illegible scrawl, saying thank you. I liked the idea of this. It was as if he had remembered the cake long after it had been eaten, and remembered who sent it, and had kept thinking how very kind it was to sent a cake across all those flat miles, and struggling to find the right words to say thank you with. This seemed so much better than the relations who one imagined scribbled out a note saying thank you ever so much for your box of chocolates, and then ate them and forgot all about them. Will would have to taste and eat the cake before saying thank you. I liked this idea of Will taking so long. It was as if the ordinary way of saying thank you wasn't good enough, and he had to find the right words, the very best words to say thank you, and not until he had found them was there any point in writing. Maybe it wasn't like this at all, but that is the way it seemed to me then, and seems to me now. I can remember once he sent by rail a great big dead bird, a pheasant or something. It stayed strung up in our kitchen for days, and I kept thinking when are we going to do something, get rid of this great big, dead ugly feathery bird. It looked a filthy thing. I had to keep going into the larder to see that it hadn't come back from the dead and started on our milk, or a nibbling through the cheese or something. It frit me to death. What the hell made him send by rail this great bloody bird. But when it was plucked and there were feathers everywhere, and then it was stuffed and cooked, it was wonderful. And I thought, that was clever of our Uncle Will, to know that after this ugly thing was done, it would be so good to eat. It was like the thank you for the Christmas cake. It was all good and great underneath, but you had to get through the mess of the feathers and the washing and stuffing and cooking, and it just being dead on a nail strung up with a bit of string; you had to get through all this before you came to the goodness. It made the taste so much more of an event, something to be remembered, and to remember Will.

I was very young when I went over there, and I was Liddie's boy. I always got the impression that our mother didn't belong in the village any more. She was the girl who went away around the country teaching and then married a man and went to live in a dirty town where they made boots and shoes and there were factories and all that. There was a conflict, I felt, with my mother and the village that didn't exist with her sister who had gone away to settle in Portsmouth, where the relations could go for holidays, and where it wasn't dirty; and the way she had become full of Pompey and the big city could be put down to the sea air. Mother I often thought half hankered back to the village; had been caught between the two having gone away for so long not being able to come back; and yet not being able to quite fit in and find roots with a town where they made things. But I loved going out there. Whenever I went to see other relations they asked what are you doing now? How you been getting on at school? — they had a load of questions that needed answers; questions kindly asked to make conversation, but I never wanted to make conversation. While out there was Uncle Will who after I'd been sitting down for ten minutes would say still at school? I'd say Yes. Then there'd be another ten minutes and then — cup of tea. There were no questions. Only statements, to which I never had to reply unless I wanted to. I liked that. It was enough for me to just be there. There were none of the painful silences I found with other relations, when you'd look at the floor and the boots and shoes and fire and keep saying to yourself — I have got to say something, make conversation, answer their kindly meant question, and I mustn't be rude. But I never wanted to say anything. If they don't know and they want me to really tell them it would take me a long time, and it wouldn't be conversation. It isn't that I'm at school, full stop. If I say that, they will go away and make conversation with other relations and say he is at school and he is getting on very nicely. No thank you, I never wanted that said. It isn't like that. If I make conversation I shall have to tell lies and half truths, and they won't get the picture at all, and that isn't fair to me or to them. There was none of this making conversation at the village. That was why I liked going over to Cambridgeshire so much. I just sat and watched the fire and the open grate, and it was alright; being quiet, no painful silence, just being quiet. You know all about the country and farming, and it would take you too long to tell me, and I'm not really interested; and the same goes the other way round, but we're relations. It was like that. It was enough to be there. There was no obligation to say anything, or make any sign, or show any interest. And the silences they were quiet, peaceful. I have my world, and you have yours. We meet because we are relations, and it is good to see your own now and then. We shall not pry. We shall keep ourselves to ourselves. If you have anything to say, or if I have anything to say we shall say it. If we have only questions we shall keep quiet. If there is any trouble of any kind, let us know, and you know we shall help you. And it was enough to be there; to show that you hadn't forgotten. I liked that. I liked that very much. I still do.

．　．　．

On the other side, my father's, it was a different world. He was brought up in Northampton. His parents, though born in the country, had lived, grown up and spent most of their lives in the town. They were a town family. Their connections with the country had disappeared. The country to them was a place you went to, or went through, but somewhere you wouldn't want to live now. On Sunday afternoons the family would go into the country in the car. Our Mum would take us for a walk along some lane, or across the fields, while Dad'd stay back in the car reading the papers. He'd catch us up later, or we'd go back to the car. It was very rare that he would ever come out of the car with us for the walk. The country to my father, and to all his side of the family is, and has been as far back as you can go over cups of tea, as remote as it is to me — best seen from a coach window, or at most reserved for the day trip.

If my mother's side is full of relations I knew but are now dead, or out of contact through my own moving on, father's side is the side of the long-lost relations. There are more than a score of relatives who get mentioned, but never written to, and never seen. They have gone away. The Gran wrote to them for a bit, but it dropped off. They went away. An aunt in Salt Lake City, an uncle in Winnipeg. Of course your uncle went out to America. Where? I forget. Do you ever write? Not now. Why not? Seems no point in it. He won't come back now, not now. Uncles and Aunts, all lost and all with great all-American families, and most of them were sisters and brothers of The Gran.

But most mysterious of all was The Gran's first husband, my grandfather who I never saw. His name was mentioned only in a whisper — the great Jimmy Gosling of The Institute and the Co-op. He was a legend, a family myth. He has seemed to me from the times when I was very young, to be the ghost the family turned to. If anyone'd know what to do now, He would. And yet, He was surrounded by a kind of black mark, as if He and not the family were responsible for his not being alive, as if He hadn't gotten killed the family wouldn't have had to scrat and save. He was the man who brought fame and money to the family, and yet there was a notoriety. He was the dark angel of the back streets where The Gran lived and kept her flower shop when I was young; a dark angel who died long before I was thought of. As a kid, I remember every time his name was mentioned, listening to catch what was said, gasping for every new bit of information to add to my picture of your Grandad.

He was a gardener by trade, working for one of the nurseries and doing odd jobs from cleaning cars to chauffeur to pick up the extra money He needed. It wasn't until after He married The Gran that He became the great figure of the legend. They lived in East Street, a street that now has a Chinese laundry and a Laundromat at the top, and is an unbroken terrace row to the disused cemetery at the bottom. It was one of a series of terrace rows now changed not only by supermarkets and landromats but by Caribbeans, American airmen, The Girls, and the OAP's. This whole block of streets running between two main roads was put up towards the end of the nineteenth and the first few years of the twentieth century, and are among the nearest Northampton has to the back to backs. They lived in one of the furthest from town streets, right in the middle. The legend says He was a wizard with figures. It was said He could make money from nothing. From what I've picked up from others who knew him, and from pubs and street-corner shops, and remarks made to me because — weren't He your Pop — it seems He was a revered figure — a bit above us — not in class or breeding, or interests but simply because He didn't seem to mix, kept hiself to hiself. In his gardening and his odd jobs He often worked for the gentry and the well-to-do but this seemed to have little effect. They weren't a white front doorstep family. There was nothing stuck up, in a class sense; but rather a keeping apart. The Gran was a go-getter, a forceful public speaker at Chapels and Co-op and The Institute, and all the other organisations that saw to it as you had your rights, you weren't done down, and were in themselves one of the finest ways out of The Street. The Gran helped to push him into public life, but in any case He was brilliant with figures. He started by getting on to the Co-op Board of Directors, with The Gran helping to swing the votes from the women's sections. Then by his being well known at the Chapels and in the Friendly Societies, and his being a respected, and I think at times feared figure from the streets he moved on and up until He finally reached the full-time paid post of Secretary to the Medical Institute. He held the post it seems like a little dictator; and in his job appeared to be ruthless, running it as a good business, and not from any guiding religious or social principles. His aim was to make it pay; to turn it into an efficient, top-grade business provided with the best drugs and the best doctors. He had no time for the Liberal Party, and the story still gets bandied around of how the town got rid of the Liberal MP — the man who lets you down. There was an election speech from the balcony of a hotel on the market square, the sitting candidate with a national leader backing him up, and the crowd got more and more wild chanting— the man as lets you down, until this national leader called the people in the square the scum, and that did it. The whole election party, including the national leader were kept in the hotel all through the night by the crowd. Your Grandfather, He was one of those that made sure the Liberal would never get back in Northampton. He did little for the Labour Party and had little time for their all-talk. And there's another favourite story, of his first days at the Institute. It was the tradition for the Chemist to the Institute to buy the drugs, and one of the first moves He made was to break with that tradition. The Secretary would buy the drugs, and the chemist's job was to dispense them, not to buy them. The story shows the type of man He was, and the way He must have made his enemies. It was through his buying of the drugs that He made connections all across the country; in Nottingham and in Ireland, and in particular down at the docks in London where He would go on Sundays, very frequently on Sundays. I have heard people say that all his buying of drugs wasn't just for the Institute. Maybe. He looked after number one. But there was never, and I have never heard anyone suggest there was, anything underhand in the way He did his job, and this I believe.

I got a snap of him in his shirt sleeves standing at the back of the house in East Street with a wry smile across his face. Where He met The Gran I don't know, though she was still in her teens when they got married. I always think of him as a tall, black and rather frightening figure getting off trams at the tram stop by the top of the street and walking slowly down those terraced rows, across the cobbles and people pulling at the lace curtains saying — He's back our gel. He's come back. He has become a legend with the family, a myth referred to with an almost religious aura. By 1931 He was rich, relatively, and powerful, and around then there was this bust up between him and The Gran, after which He left her and took rooms further out of town. I don't think He was ever a popular man, or a very good man; but I think He knew his oats backwards, how to run a business. One of the greatest disgraces I found myself with is being the first one in the family, as far back as anyone can remember who has been in debt.

By 1931 He knew what was what with money, people, local politics, business. He seemed to have little regard for the traditional beliefs and taboos. He didn't smoke and He didn't drink. But He travelled on Sundays. He wasn't a great Chapel man, but He went. He had his ways and means, bought and sold, and made money, didn't do anything for nothing. And in 1932 He was killed. Some say it was murder; some manslaughter, some an accident. In 1932 He was killed outright by a motor car. The whole business was strange. The driver of the car was an old enemy. And after He died strange things happened. The Coroner's inquest was got through as quick as possible. Night after night a man would wait below the house in East Street, just hang around by the gaslamp, every night till well after midnight. All his papers were burned at the Institute. The funeral at the Chapel was full, to capacity, with all the Chapel, Co-op, Institute attending. Pictures were taken by the papers of the mourners, and none got published. One policeman admitted at the inquest that things weren't quite in order. People disappeared, and left town. A house everyone knew He owned had been sold a few days before He died, but there was no trace of any documents, money, or anything. There was nothing in his pockets when they picked him up. Solicitors He dealt with went dumb and said nothing, said they knew nothing. There was nothing The Gran could actually put the finger on, but something smelt fishy. They weren't sure who they could trust, solicitors, police, Chapel, Co-op. Everyone seemed to have been mixed up in things the last few days before He died. And no one would say anything. For The Gran and the family down at East Street the whole business must have been one long drawn-out agony, shock on shock — after all the rows, his walking out of the house and taking rooms, and then only a week or so later being knocked down by a motor car. He had always been a man who kept himself to himself. No one knew all the things He did; how much money He made, where He went. There were so many blanks about him that even The Gran didn't know. What happened to his money? Did He really have any? I don't know. I'm only his grandson. All I have to go on is the family legend. But I have walked into shops and offices in this town and announced myself and seen old men turn white, look just like death. Did you ever know a man called Jimmy Gosling, you see I'm his grandson and ... — and the door has been closed in my face. I've been told to let sleeping dogs lie, and perhaps it's best that way. But the legend, it's got passed on to me and it's made the impact. I believe He made money. I believe He was a man who wouldn't mix with any local chit chat. The legend with its guilts, and suspicions, has been passed on to me, and I've made out my own theories; the legend of this austere, strange, silent man who got killed by his own stubbornness, other people's jealousy—I wouldn't know, yet.

I can remember as a little boy in a tweed coat with a belt that I loved because it was so warm and had a bit of class about it, and was different from everybody else's going down to Sunday roast at The Gran's in East Street, and the relations sitting round the fire after dinner and talking away. They did nothing but talk, talk, talk and I'd sit all quiet in the dark stuffy room, taking it all in, and then someone'd say—he's like his Pop isn't he, our George's boy—and I felt this wasn't only praise or petting, or even statement. It were like a curse, like for better or for worse and you can bet you boots it'll be worse. I've always had, ever since I can remember, this idea of the second time round. Like grandfather, like grandson, second novel, second time of seeing a person, a film, a play, reading a book. It's not the first that really counts, but the second. It's a daft idea, that wastes time, but it's made the— like his grandad—stick all the more.

And there was The Gran, and the flower shop. After He died, and she began to find her feet again. She turned the front room into a flower shop. She had to to make ends meet. They were near the cemetery which was until a few years ago a going concern, and she made wreaths and crosses and sold daffs and sweets and cigs. There was no previous experience, but the gamble paid off. It had to. The only sign last time I walked down the street of the old shop was a fading chipped tin sign for Wills' Star cigarettes standing over the coal hole, and the extra large front window, and a few rusty iron forks sticking out from the wall where The Gran would hang the wreaths and pots and bunches of flowers. Now, it's one of the shabbiest houses in the street, but to me it's still the flower shop, one of my most vivid childhood memories; the flowers and the smell and The Gran talking and talking and talking. She was a little woman, and always seemed crowded out by the flowers and boxes and tins of stuff in the front shop, or the darkness of the back room, or the back yard piled high with flower boxes and empties and she never stopped talking — on and on — proud, arrogant, kind, and supremely confident. There was no feeling of belonging to the working classes, or even of belonging to the streets. They were there. That was all. The flower shop was the way out. Make your money, enough to get out, enough to move on. That was it. She was a wonderful little woman, and I think it must have been from her and the legend of Him that I got much of my own stubbornness, my feeling of no one's going to grind me down. I shall fight and fight my way out and on forwards, but I shall not forget, and I shall fight from where I stand, from where I belong, on the ground.

After my grandfather died, my father became the bread-winner. The Gran did marry later on, though her second husband never came alive to me. Whenever the family talk came round to Jimmy Gosling and the first few years after He died I could always sense the swallowing of some bitter pill. There was my Dad, self-educated, inheriting the books and the public speaking and the urge to get on and get out, and the friends from the Co-ops, and Chapels, and at the Institute: Doctors, and Ministers, and Politicians — and all this, and all the possibilities of doing everything, and the glorious future and then when He died the future just vanished, because He had kept so much to himself and it died with him. Now life meant little more than scraping together enough to keep the home going. The promise and the future had been levelled down to the present and the breadline. It must have been painful for the family in those few years after He died. He had always said—when I die you'll be alright. And then He was dead, and there was nothing, no will; less than nothing, the faces turned away at Chapel, the people who wouldn't speak. Dad mended motor bikes and then motor cars and kept up as best he could the books and the reading and the speaking; but it must have been clear that it wouldn't be for his future. I was very conscious of this; that the way out, the next moves on were my job; that I had to pick up the threads where He left off, and where Dad couldn't go. The chance and the opportunity and the hopes of the family were to rest with me. No one ever said this, but it was the line I picked up, though the point never got forced on me. They hoped I would take the hint. There was never any pressure from them. My father's sister, she stayed at home in East Street with the books and all that, and worked and worked and passed exam on exam all off her own bat until she became a fully qualified elocution and piano, and then general teacher. But by being shut away and having to work so hard in such wretched conditions; going out and away the tough way without being able to use the recognised paths, and with all the inevitable loss of social contact, her success was never the It. The Gran though always saying she's done so well and now teaching she is at a great big school on the south coast. Yes, she's done well but it wasn't the real thing. She worked too hard. The family, they had to swallow a great lump when I, the one who'd been given every chance and every opportunity to get on, came out of a free university place without finishing the course. That was a big one to swallow.

.   .   .

My parents met at the Malvern Festival. Mum had gone over with friends, while father went to see the Shaw plays and the Barry Jackson productions, and he loved the theatre. They met and met again after Malvern and became engaged, and then both of them saved up until they could afford to get married. And then they were married, and Mum gave up teaching and moved into Northampton where they rented a house, still saving up enough to put down for a mortgage on a new house. They wanted a home more than anything else; a home fit to bring children into and give them every chance. They both made great sacrifices, and there was so much given up for the sake of the children that whenever I've gone off the conventional rails I have had terrible qualms, and had to argue it out with myself point by point whether I was doing the fair thing by them, what my reasons were. For Dad the children were the great hope, and for both of them the security they saved up for was not really for them, but for the children. I was the first, and arrived in 1939. It was, so I've been told, a great struggle to keep me alive in the first few days. I wasn't easy at all. It seems I just wouldn't make the effort to live. But with the help of doctors and friends, and sleepless nights and parents I came through and was a fat happy baby just in time for war to be declared. Father was a volunteer and joined up with the R.E.M.E.,* or its equivalent before the war was actually declared. He was the second in our street to go off. His idea was to get in first, and as long as he had any choice keep as near to home as he could. Mother didn't go out to work, but we took in evacuees from London. I think there was an old couple, and some kids and then some more old couples.

But my memories of the war are very vague. I can remember sitting in the shelters the night Coventry was bombed, and coming out and being held up to see the red glow in the sky to the west, and being told — Coventry's gone. I can remember the *Daily Express* headlines and the feel of the newspaper, and its smell; and Dad coming home tired after hitching through the night from Wilts or Yorks, and the smell of khaki and his only being home a few hours before he went off on the road back. I can remember clothing coupons, but I can't remember Hitler or Churchill or Dunkirk, or the Blitz, or rationing. I can remember an aeroplane with a black cross on its side coming down in a field a little way from home, and running out to see it, and there was the fire brigade and the police, and ambulances all over the place, but this memory has been merged, like in a dream, with a memory of crawling through a tunnel of snow on the hill to get to the village during one of the very bad winters. I remember the old red buses with their wooden seats, and going down to see The Gran on Sundays, and good Aunt Ada with her shock of white hair coming up to see us. I remember when there was no housing estate at the bottom of our garden, but a field of

---

* Royal Electrical and Mechanical Engineers, a British Army regiment.

corn and a blackbird nest, and an orchard at the bottom of the road and only three shops at the top of the street, and the nearest Co-op being right down the hill towards the town; and going down to the little village church, coming in with mother once after walking all the mile and a half from home just as the vicar was giving the blessing and creeping in with mother at the back and people looking at us as if we had committed a crime against the state by coming into church, a church a quarter full in any case, too late. It must be, I thought because we missed the collection. I can remember the V.E. party at the top of the street with the flags all out, and me thinking, thinking so they think it's all over, but they're still fighting out in Japan, and all the people who won't come back like the man who went in before our Dad, and there's still the clothing coupons. But I can't remember The Bomb or Hiroshima or Nagasaki.

I remember being sent away when it was time for my sister to be born into a village in Huntingdonshire where there were relations. I was terrified and we kept punting down this beautiful river. I hated being away. I cried and cried to go back. I was very conscious of something very important happening back at home, and I was there in this stupid lovely village, with these relations who kept asking me questions, trying to make me feel at home. All I wanted was to be left alone, and to wander by the river, and draw pictures of the church by the river and the willows, the church without a steeple or a tower; but no — they wouldn't let me. They wanted me to be happy and to feel at home. I didn't want to be happy, or to feel at home. I was away. I hated it. I was so glad to get back into Northampton, back into the town, and then seeing this little thing all quiet and wrapped up in a shawl in a pram in the hall, and being so wonderfully happy at being back at home, and that this after all was all I'd been sent away for. I liked the idea of this furry, funny little thing all wrapped up. I liked the idea of there being another. And I was glad to be back where there were buses and houses and lavatories that flushed and lots and lots of people.

And I remember the holidays, perhaps more than anything, the goings away — Leicester and London and being taken away from one holiday because I was ill and having to be rushed home and the doctor coming up in a hurry and having my neck cut open. I felt bad. Thought I'd never live again. It was very hot. Had something taken out. Don't know what it was. It was hot and steamy and the sun shone through the curtains, and I was all wrapped up with poultices and it went on for days and days, just lying on my back in bed while it was all hot outside.

And then there was the first real holiday at Hunstanton just after the war. The place was all dirty and very grim. It looked as if a war had really been going on. I can remember the sand and thinking of all the terrible things that had been done — the barbed wire and the broken pier — and how nice it must have been before those things came, the war and all that; how everything had been ruined except the sand. I remember screaming all the way home in this hot steamy non-corridor train, all the way home.

After that we went down south, Portsmouth. Seeing whole streets left with just stumps of buildings and our Aunt Annie all fat and happy and sun tanned and cheerful coming down the steps at Fratton Park station to meet us, and hearing how they got bombed out three times and it didn't mean a thing. But their tortoise, he survived it all and I thought how wonderful the tortoise was, surviving all those bombs and the fire and the war. I'd stroke his hard shell and feel the softness beneath the shell, and think how he must have been guided by some god, or good spirit or something to have come through all that; and I'd run my finger over his shell and think — all those ruins on top of you, and you're still alive. I remember walking with Annie along the front and through the centre and her saying before the war there was this ... and before the war ... before the war and all I could see were the stumps of shops, office blocks, houses, streets, piers, just stumps. But there were the trolley buses with their wires above the streets where there was nothing left but rubble and stumps, and it was alright. There they were, the only sign left intact of what there once was, these thin swaying wires above the road. We went across to the Isle of Wight for the day, and I liked that. And there was Hastings, and Skegness for the day, and everywhere there was one constant: there had been a war.

We went to Bournemouth one year, and that was alright. The place we stayed at — they said it overlooked the sea, and they were quite right, but it took a threepenny bus ride to get to it. We felt we'd been done down, and so after a few days we moved out to a great big mansion place in the country where we never saw the sea, but it wasn't so far to get at. It was alright out there. There was this great big orchard, and a garden swing and the whole place looked as if it was falling down, and it wasn't because of the war. It was all old and musty and derelict with that peculiar smell like a Tennessee Williams country. I liked it there, a natural falling off and falling apart: no war.

I can remember standing on Waterloo station waiting for a train to Pompey and I was ever so small and there was a big horrible Cockney woman who must have had a wart on the end of her nose. Stood there all loud and vulgar telling our Mum all about how with their being so much polio about I'd be sure to catch it and it was a great big sin it was for them to be taking me on a holiday with all that about, and how it served them right if I went and caught it and died, but of course she hoped I'd be lucky and miss it, but the chances were that I'd catch it and die, and how mum and dad ought to be ashamed of themselves taking me away with all that about. And I wanted to hit her, so hard. You stand there with your superior airs, your superior cockney airs thinking we don't have radios and newspapers where we live. We've heard all about this polio and we know the risk and the precautions to take, but we're going on holiday. We want this holiday, scrat and saved we have and looked forward to it, all the year we have. Don't ruin it for us. Let us go and make the most of it, it's the only one we have. I tell you if you were cooped up in a place like Northampton you'd want to get out of it for just the one week of the year, polio or no polio; and in any case what are *you* doing going down there with all that about. And I remember having tea on the train and spilling it and our Mum laughing and our Dad telling me it was naughty and a woman sitting eating her cake and staring at us funny little people making such a stir about spilling tea on a railway table-cloth. And there was the time we went down by road, and we parked the car outside this café, and when we came out we found the car had gone, and we looked all around and then we found it all squashed in a parking zone, removed by the police and I thought that was good. They hadn't stuck a label on the window, or arrested us as we came out but quietly towed it away; and we had thought ourselves so good driving right up to the door of this café, and parking this tatty little red convertible right outside this big posh café. Those holidays were wonderful. I shall always be grateful for those days.

But there were other things, though holidays were best. There was the Panto at the theatres at Christmas. I loved the Panto. There was the films and going with our Mum to see Henry the Fifth. There was Christmas with The Gran coming up just in time to eat the chicken, and then the pudding with the holly on top and the silver coins inside, and the nuts, and the presents, and the stockings; and our Mum having just a drop of sherry and a cigarette because it was Christmas. I was very happy. There was always something to look forward to, dreams came true, everything was nice and all holidays and laughing. I liked it then.

I can remember prisoners of war. I think they were Italians, all sitting round an open fire at the end of a lane near us, and I was all on my own, and I went all fascinated and interested and not really afraid across to them and they laughed and smiled and talked foreign and they picked me up over this fire, all of them hadn't had a shave and had those beards. Whenever I see a picture of Castro's Cuba I think of those POW's. I liked them, but couldn't understand why they didn't run away. There was no barbed wire and they seemed free enough, not at all like the photos in the papers. I liked them, being all foreign and laughing. There was a slab of concrete along where they just built this new school and it has written on it a name and a P.O.W. number. When I was older I'd go and look at this slab and think of how kind they were and wonder where they were now, and what they were doing now it was all over. I couldn't understand why we wanted to fight and kill them. They seemed alright, all bearded and foreign and laughing, and they were ever so kind to me. If that was war I didn't like it.

But in the end I had to go to school. This for me was the first time I became conscious of things being not quite right and fair in the concrete and personal sense. There was a school and a good one just over fifty yards up our street on the same side as us. I naturally thought I'd be going there. I used to sit in this toy car that our Dad had made for me, all hand-made with bicycle pedals to move it along, much faster and bigger than the ones in the shops, and listen to the singing of the hymns from the assembly at the school; and meet the big boys when they came out of school and give them a lift on my bonnet down to the bus stop. It was something to look forward to, going to the big school. But our house was in the Rural District, and the school was in the town. Our back fence was the boundary line. But on our side of the street five doors up the boundary twisted and became the front fence of the houses, so the houses and the school that were only five doors from us were in the town. As we were in the Rural I had to go to the village school which was over a mile and a half from our house, down in the village and across the big dangerous trunk road that separated the estates from the village proper. Our Dad said I wouldn't go to the village school, and the whole business was daft. He said I went to the town school or I went to no school. The Rural people came round and said that in that case I would go to no school, and that was against the law, and so I would have to go to the village school. All the people on the Rural side of the street came and met at our house and agreed to stand together and fight for their kids to go to the town school. The battle went on for over a year and nearly two, and by the time it ended we were the only ones holding out against the Rural. During this time I was taught how to read and write and do sums by our Mum who was a teacher before in any case. She taught me very well. Every time the school's inspector came round our Dad kept him standing on the doorstep while he argued it out with him, and he'd go away saying — I'll have you sued — and Dad'd say — Go on, then, do something, sue me then, just try it on — and in the end they let me in at the town school. But by this time I didn't want to go to school anywhere. I was happy at home being taught by our Mum. The first day I went I ran away. I hated it. I was older than the others, more advanced than many of my own age; and they moved me from class to class until they found the right stream for me, and they made me go over everything mother had taught me. The result was that, either from wanting to be different or from sheer bad teaching, I mucked up most of what I should have learnt and forgot most of what our Mum had taught me, and soon I could neither spell, or write, or read or do sums. I was a backward child after a year at school. When the time came for grading at the end of the Infants I was bottom of the A grade. I wouldn't mix with the snotty-nosed lot from the town council houses. I didn't know any of the nicer people from the other town estates. I was the only county boy; and I wasn't clever. I hated that place. Through infant school I was the odd boy out, and a naughty boy. But as the time for moving into the Juniors came I was joined by other county boys; I was finding a few nice friends and a friend whose home had television, and I was beginning to settle in. And then I broke my arm. Nothing unusual in that. It was plastered up and put in a sling, and got better and then I broke it again. Through the Juniors it broke once, two, three, four, six, eight times and this was not really right. It wasn't nice at all. I had The Arm, and that changed about everything.

. . .

The first time I broke my arm I went to the doctor and then down to the hospital and there was an X-ray. I was treated for a fracture. I came back with The Arm in plaster and a sling, and it got better again. But then I fell off my bike, or tripped on a paving stone and it would break again, and again. Well, after about the fourth break the hospital became a little concerned. There might, they thought, be more to The Arm than a simple fracture. I broke it again, and they were sure there was more than a simple fracture, or even a multiple. It seems a shame that I had to keep breaking it before they found out something was wrong. At first the attraction of having a plaster arm people could write their names on, countered that of not being able to play games and all that, but after breaking it time and time again I had become the County boy who was a bit silly and kept breaking his arm. All of my little idiosyncracies and differences were enlarged by being the boy with The Arm, the special one, the odd one out.

Eventually they took me into hospital for an operation at the beginning of a December and I remember screaming and screaming — I was not going to eat their porridge. I was not going to eat their porridge. They were determined I should. And one morning before any patients were awake, as the dawn was coming in, I was smartly wheeled down a corridor into a room. One nurse held me on to the bed, and there in front was a great big steaming hot bowl of porridge. Another nurse came from behind and opened my mouth, and the third came smiling towards me with this very first spoonful of the good stuff. I went crazy, and fought, and screamed and with the good arm I got hold of the plate of steaming good stuff and threw it at the nurses, the wall, the bed and gave them back their bloody porridge. After that I was permitted to have flakes with milk, and I liked that. While I was waiting for Operation Day I was free to wander through the wards. I can remember one that was full of war wounded, people all half dead beneath and above pink blankets trying to laugh and joke with me and trying to read the papers. It was horrible. They weren't the young who'd recover, or the old who'd die; but they were men and they would have to live with half legs and half faces, and lie between the pink blankets and try to read the papers, and laugh and joke and make the best of that. I felt bad about this because I was, as far as they could see, as healthy as anyone could be. It made it much worse my not looking ill, or about to have an operation.

After a few days I was wheeled away and painted so that the skin nearly all over me looked like Danish blue cheese; all yellowy-blue, green — all the sickly colours. On the next day the doctors came to see me before breakfast, and I was given a pill that made me go all dreamy and then I was wheeled along this dark long corridor, and the double swing doors at the end seemed to get closer and closer towards me, and opened automatically it seemed as we got on top of them, and I lay on a table, and there were arc lamps all above and doctors and nurses and knives and someone said — breathe — and I breathed and passed out way beyond. I really thought I'd never come through alive. And while I was out they cut open my side and took a piece of bone from my hip, and then cut open my arm and scraped all the bad away and put in this piece of hip bone they had taken from my side; and I was wheeled back and when I woke I found I was alive and covered in plaster all over. They told me to lie still but there was so much plaster I couldn't move, but I was so glad to be back alive I think I would even have taken the porridge, but they were very kind, and I kept to my cornflakes. I liked cornflakes, then. I came out of hospital three days before Christmas. I must have been in three weeks to a month. When the time came to start school again I was ready. But at school I was now treated with care, as a delicate child, as a special case by the staff, with no PT or games. The awful thing about The Arm was that I looked and felt just the same as everybody else. I didn't look ill, or delicate, and I never felt it.

One night I was out with a crowd from the streets and we went up to a big private estate that was all illegal to go to. If they ever found you on it they chased you with a gun. There was a lake there, and a boathouse, and sweet schoolchildren would blow up frogs they caught at the side of the lake. Put a straw in the frog's mouth and blow until it comes up like a balloon, and then prick it with a pin so it burst. This was a sort of epidemic that grew to serious proportions, with warnings from the police and schools about children who were caught blowing up frogs, and the place being illegal. There was a statue there, a statue of a man wrestling with some animal in a field on the estate it was. This particular night I was with this crowd fooling around by the statue, and I being the delicate child at school was not going to be done down out of school as well, so we were having some sort of game seeing who could climb on to the top of the statue and balance for the greatest length of time without falling off. Well I climbed it, and to the cheers of the crowd of kids I stood on one leg with both arms in the air at the very top of the statue, and I bowed to the crowd and fell, and I broke my arm. It was all rather rich. I was carried home in state. The Arm had gone again. They wouldn't let me walk. I had to be carried. Then I went to the doctors, and then to the hospital, and they all stood around and shook their heads. It was serious. The bad in The Arm was still there. The operation was not a success, and I felt guilty then about not taking my porridge. Our Dad was called in and the situation was explained and the suggestion was made that a simple amputation of the whole arm might be a solution. The Arm was going for good. I didn't like that. They didn't like it at home either. I'd grown attached to The Arm. People would say what a healthy boy I was, and it was a great source of pride to be able to think — yes, but they don't know of the bad in The Arm. Well our Dad went down to the hospital and told all the doctors that he didn't believe them, and that if all they could think of was having my arm off then they weren't much good, and so he went round to another department of the hospital. He found a doctor who said — The Arm, I cure The Arm for you. You should have seen me first. I cure The Arm for you — yes? — and our Dad said yes, and The Arm was cured. For day after day, for month on month I lay on a black bed under a black machine that purred away all alone while a group of nurses sat behind a glass wall and flicked switches and lights changed colour, and the big black machine kept purring away, and they killed the bad in The Arm, and made sure that The Arm would never be bad any more.

The doctor was a foreigner, and everything a foreigner should be. He was Russian, a Pole, a Jew, a little man, clever, loud voice and thick accent; everything I thought of as being of the enemy he had; that mixture of Black, German, Russian, Jew. He was one of the kindest and greatest men I've ever come across. He was a dealer in the dying, the dead: cancer. For day after day I sat with the old and the hopeless waiting for The Doctor to come. It was far worse than the war wounded ward at the hospital where I had the operation, for there they were like that because of the war. It wasn't the war that brought the people to The Doctor. They were dying, not in constant state of half-dead. Theirs was a living pain, a thing that grew until it took you over, and you had to die. The Doctor was honest and truthful, and he knew his job and his people — doctor will it?... I don't know, we may stop it in time — and once — you are going to die I tell you. All I can do is ease the pain. I do that. You have no pain. I have never seen so many old, and hopeless and poor and they were all treated alike. My arm was cured but it left two very deep scars, two memories I couldn't forget, and leave as a part of the past;

two deep impressions that have become like a cancer, a part of me. The Arm, bone, structure was cured but in the process I caught a taste, it'll always be with me, always.

There I sat with the old, and the lost and the forgotten and the slow dead, and it made me feel in a way, guilty. I was the only young one there. I was the only one who looked alright. I was often the only one there who looked alive, living. And to make it worse there was nothing you could see. I sat in my blazer and no one could see anything wrong with The Arm. They couldn't see it, but I knew it was there. And I kept on thinking — I'm going to get better. I hold the cards. I got the chances. I don't look ill. I don't even feel ill. And they looked at me, kept on looking at me as if I was some intruder or something and I'd ask them, not knowing how cruel I could be — what's the matter luv? what brings you here? and they'd say — He's a good doctor. He's doing his best. It stops the pain. There isn't much they can do. I'm getting on now. They do what they can — and sometimes they'd stare straight into the wall and say — I got a growth — It took a long while for the message to get through, but in the end I understood. It was ... cancer. I had to go there day after day for weeks and it bit deep; just sitting there sometimes talking about the weather. They used to smile; the resignation; the poor; the acceptance. And they'd tell me — people, they don't want to know me now. The doctor he says it aint catching, but they don't believe me. I like that doctor. He doesn't run away. It all made me feel I wanted to crawl under the floorboards, because it was my sort, the sort that looked alright that were the ones who did the running away. I made up my mind. I wasn't going to run away. I think it was one of the first things, one of my very first experiences that made up my mind: I belong down here, sitting and waiting. I don't belong up there at the school where they're all laughing and where they don't care a bloody damn. Poverty and pain, when they go together; it's like you got hit right between the eyes by the hardest man in the Town. I looked just like everybody else from the outside, but I told them about The Arm and I was alright. I was on their side. It was where I wanted to be, and it was enough to just be there.

But it did something else to me. You can't see that one arm is shorter than the other, but I know that it is. I know that if I roll up my sleeves you'll see it. I'm still very conscious of this. Self-conscious over this arm. It's as if I carried the plague around with me, something bad, some bad seed, something that you can't see and you won't know about; but I know it's there. All the time I know it's there. I know that you could see it if only I took my shirt off. I want to tell you, take my shirt off so you'll see this thing I carry around with me; but I daren't. And so I carry the thing around with me, and I want to show you, but I don't so you don't know, but I know and that makes me into some sort of cheat, a fraud. That's what it does to you, a thing like that. People they say—Oh don't be silly. There's nothing to worry about. Just act normal. That sort of talk, it makes me sick. Of course I act normal, explaining to my tailor not to forget the inch difference in my suiting. But to me, it's there, and it's a thing. I don't ever worry about it, worry, not now; but I am always aware of it, conscious of it being there. And it cut out sports and games for me, just like that. It wasn't that I couldn't play. It was just that if I took my shirt off, it was there. The Arm. And it affected me throughout, not just with sport. There's that poem by Auden, goes—

> *Lay your sleeping head, my love,*
> *Human on my faithless arm*

It's taken me years to get used to it, just being there. Making sure you slept on the right side of the bed; making sure you didn't get touched on that side—and all the while the thought—has she seen, has

he noticed. It's not so bad now; but even now I know it's there.

Physically it's never hindered me in any way at all. I've never really wanted to play sports or anything like that. It's never stopped me from doing what I wanted to do, but it's made me feel left out, a little. Because even if I had wanted to, would I have dared? Over the years I've added to my collection of scars, and black eyes, and twisted toes, and funny legs and pains all over and all sorts of things but there has never been anything like The Arm. It's funny in a way. I see an old friend at a bar, and I look and they look, and I smile and I know and they know. With some people it's become a sort of secret link, something found out by accident in the middle of the night. I wouldn't want to lose it, not now, because it's special, exclusive and all that.

It's also had the reverse effect at times. I'm a bad scrapper, and I'm a fast loser. I don't like physical violence, but when it comes I've never been scared of finishing up in the casualty for the night, The Arm or no arm. It has made me turn like that; another cog to the wheels of defiance, stubbornness, rebellion. In spite of this I shall go on. This isn't going to stand in my way, not one little bit. I remember going down to Brighton one Sunday from London, all on my own, just because I felt like it, and one of the boys back in London got picked up by the bogeys, and the rest of the boys thought I'd grassed on him, and down they came to Brighton to find me, and they found me. There was no way of proving I hadn't grassed. That has been the only time I have thought, and had time to think — I'm going to get hurt, damn this arm why isn't it right? Normally, though, it doesn't worry me, physically. I know it's there. All the time I'm conscious of it. Can't get rid of it. It's just one of those things, fits into this jigsaw — me as I now am; and it's one of the things that happened in this place.

This arm business took me through junior school and the first half of grammar school, but something happened in between that had nothing to do with The Arm. I passed the 11 plus and it was considered by all including myself to be something of a miracle. The headmaster of that junior school, he told my mother right to her face that I had no hope of passing as I had been a naughty boy, and rather silly, and had come forty-eighth out of forty-eight in the class and wasn't very bright, and there had been this arm. There was no hope whatsoever, but I passed. When people talk about the 11 plus I remember that. It was agony, and having to take the exam for the County while the rest of the school took the town one and having to walk all the way down to the village school and having to sit with people from the villages all around and how the invigilators and the pupils took a delight in snubbing one for attending the town school, and coming out with their nasty hopes that you'd get put in your place when you failed as you'd have then to go to a County school. At eleven it was all very frightening. The results from the town came through about a month before ours, and there seemed so long to wait that I had almost forgotten; and I remember coming up the street and seeing one of the kids running down the street and saying the results are in and you've passed. I think I may have fainted or something. I was to go to the great big town and county grammar school. Everyone was very proud of me, and I was very proud of myself, and even the school — they hoped I wouldn't come forty-eighth out of forty-eight at the big school.

What was I like at eleven? The Arm was just something that was funny ha ha, it's broken again our Mum. What was I like at eleven? I tell you, stupid, stuck up; but then I think that if I'd lost then some of my silly bits, then now I'd be teaching, or something safe and worthwhile and everybody would be proud of me. Cut this one down will you, let's get some detail: say something — what were you like at eleven?

four

I WAS A LITTLE GRAMMAR SCHOOL BOY, WHAT THEY
used to call a grammar grub who had been brought up right
and nice. I was a little arkub, and I knew the difference
between what was nice and what was naughty. Maybe my
daddy was only a motor mechanic, but he was a skilled motor
mechanic and his was an important job. Maybe my granny
did come from the back streets, but she wasn't like the
common people. She had a little shop. I was a nice little boy. I
had passed the exam and I was to go to The School, and it was
a very old school, fifteen hundred and something; and I
didn't go to the dirty pictures on a Saturday morning. No,
I watched the television at a friend's and his father was a
manager. I knew what was wrong with Britain: all them
people like Lord Pakenham,* calls himself a Lord but I know
better. He's a Roman Catholic and a Socialist. It wasn't at all
nice for a Lord to be a Socialist. It wasn't; and if a Lord was a
Roman Catholic as well, he must be immoral and a revolutionary, a dreadful, very naughty man. I knew where I was
going: three steps into the future and a car, a nice wife, a first
child, selling leather and going home to our bungalow; no
worker's life for this one.

---

* Francis Pakenham, later know as Lord Longford. Life Peer and former
government minster.

I wasn't bright academically, and this wasn't helped by my feeling slightly superior. Once again I felt the disadvantage of having a school teacher for a mother and a father with a front room full of books. In the front room were the collected works of every major poet and Shakespeare and Shaw and Wilde. And of course I wasn't the type of boy who should have access to such books. I was by the record a working-class boy. Our Dad for all the skilled part was a manual worker, in a garage and not an office. But I had just written a play, nearly all in verse, and there was The Railway Club.

When I was very small I had a train set, just like every other boy, but my train set like the pedal car was home-made — partly because we couldn't afford a new set, and partly because our Dad could make one as good if not better than the ones for sale in the shops. From this first railway set, I built with our Dad's help a complicated garden railway system. It was permanent, complete with concrete viaducts, stations with glass roofs and electric lighting and real live steam engines. We had what we thought of as a vast garden, though in fact it was about the usual size for a semi-detached house of the 1930's, and this railway covered a large amount of ground with over ten stations and a tunnel under the rockery. The whole thing was home-made, from the rails themselves to some of the engines. Most of the kids from the street and around came along to help, and the interest was converted into a proper club. The railway never worked perfectly, but the whole of the enthusiasm lay in the building of the railway not in its operation. As soon as we had finished and perfected one section we would decide to knock it down and start again in a different way. It was a constant experiment; making concrete, and track and trains. From this we moved into the loco-spotting field. Some of us belonged to a local club run by a good-hearted schoolteacher with the help of one of the commercial organisations. We began to take over his club. I found a rochety old typewriter in our loft and wrote pompous letters to Motive Power Superintendents on the railway saying could our members visit train sheds, and then throw in the blah blah blah education line, that was necessary to get a permit.

The first trip was mismanaged. I found I had planned to make a train connection between two places on a train that didn't exist. Not to be outdone the party of about fifteen stopped a brick lorry and we hitched to just make the train connection for the next part of the trip. The club grew until it became larger than its commercially-sponsored rival. After the first fiasco the trips ran more smoothly with twenty, thirty, forty kids roaming engine sheds and works collecting train numbers while Shedmasters searched for this educational man who runs the trips; the Man who wrote the letters. There was London and Derby and Leeds, and the climax was a mammoth trip to Crewe Works where the supervision was strict and only by doing the wildest pity us poor little children act in front of the Gaffer were we allowed to go on the tour of inspection. He told me — did I know that no one was supposed to take the tour under eighteen. I assured him that no one was under seventeen at any road. He said he'd find out. He went into the corridor, and says to this kid — how old are you — the kid says just fourteen-that made the day, but we got round. The trips were chaotic, and there were the usual petty acts of vandalism on the train back in our reserved coach. As we grew older the club faded away. And in any case I'd got into a financial muddle with the enterprise, partly because I tried to run the trips at a ridiculously low operating cost, making them as cheap as they could be for the kids, and because I was spending the money before I actually had it. This meant that whenever I made a slip up I had to borrow and scrounge to pay back what 1 should have kept, but had already spent. But it did one thing for me. I soon enough found out that I didn't like the better children and was happy, pleased, to take sides with the vandals and see the better children frightened away. While all this was going on I was moving, twelve, thirteen, fourteen, and I was changing. As I began to overcome any sense of shyness I was finding myself more at ease with the wild ones, the lunatic fringe from the secondary moderns, than with the nicer children round who the whole idea had started. And through the trips there was the love of places that rapidly replaced any interest in engines; the shape of towns, the types of streets, the sound of local accents; these had begun to fascinate me.

At the end of the first year at school there was a grading exam after which one moved into either A for arts, or B for science, or C for not so good, or D for dunces. I went into C, and once there into the lunatic fringe. When the head-master spoke of the hooligan and lunatic fringe in our midst, that was us. When the ball went that way, I went the other. When the others played rugger, we were in the Town, our macks covering our blazers, our hats in our pockets, our ties off, listening to the juke box and drinking tea. When the others on Speech Day listened to the speeches in crowded rooms through the relay system we were in a deserted hut playing cards. By the time we reached the fifths we were spending the cricket season drinking and smoking and talking beyond the cricket fields, and the woods, alongside a canal that ran right outside the school grounds. I remember after we'd been caught drinking and smoking by the river our form master coming in on the following morning and saying the headmaster has just told me that he found a crowd of fifth formers drinking and smoking and heaven only knows what else down by the river when they should have been playing cricket. I assured him that none of them could have come from this class, and that they must have come from the bottom stream — and then, right then, the headmaster's boy came in and read out a list of names the headmaster wanted to see over the incident and every name was from our class. He, the form master, had just finished saying that what happens to them should be a lesson to us more intelligent ones, when the boy came in to read out the names. He looked so sad. I used to feel sorry so sorry, for him; his inexhaustible confidence in the decency of his class.

Only two subjects interested me, and in these two and only these two I could come right to the top — English and Geography. Geography fascinated me, just the look of maps and places and people. And for English I shall always be grateful to one teacher, just one. English was something that not only went through the syllabus and on to Osborne and Kerouac and Auden, but further to cover the world we lived in; a combined history, sociology, geography and local news-everything not only that people did put down on paper, but that which they might; what they and we saw, heard, thought, felt. The Romantics were avoided and the Augustans encouraged. I liked that. And there were the school plays — son to MacDuff in *Macbeth*, Monk No. 2 in Auden's *F6*. And there was stuff we wrote ourselves — the only prize I ever won, a Poetry prize and then they'd only print one of them in the school magazine — the others were declared obscene; yet really they were all very respectable. The wonderful thing was they never laughed at you, not that way, you know.

From the lunatic fringe only two survived into the sixth-form. The rest went off into the Army, the Navy, labouring, and some just went out of town and no one heard of them again. But I wanted to go into the sixth-form. After the others had given their reasons for going into the sixth — university, good job, tradition, teaching, daddy, vocation — I could only say that I wanted to read more books and look at more maps full stop. They were very nice about this, and said that if, if I obtained the required number of 'O' level passes, they'd consider me. There was, of course, no chance of me doing this, after all I spent all my time drinking and smoking and hanging round juke-box cafés. But I came through, smiling, on top, surprisingly well, gained my place.

Through the railway club, and through getting and being a part of the lunatic fringe I discovered that The School was not me. Lord behold us with thy blessing once again assembled here: and at the Coronation being presented with *Elizabeth Our Queen* by Richard Dimbleby: the Old Boys Dinner and Dance — no I didn't and wasn't going to force myself to like that. The whole business was phoney. I soon found out that childhood friends from the nice estate were taught to look down on me — that terribly funny little boy, but rather inferior child, it's quite a shame. I might live in a semi-detached house and all that, but my parents were poor. I got worse than other kids whose parents hadn't saved to buy a semi-detached. We invaded their estates. The fact that my parents were poor, and working didn't reach me till I was at least thirteen. I hated The School. I hated the district I lived in. I loved the front room at home with all the books, and the old typewriter. I loved the juke-box caffs and the pubs. There was a spontaneity and a common equality that didn't extend to The School where the spontaneity didn't exist, and the friendship offered was under certain non-human conditions, and worse of all where you had no dignity, no person.

And there were the commitments. I remember at the 1951 General Election having a furious argument with someone of the same age and from our street at The School. I could not understand how he could stick up for the Labour. The future and the chances for the 11-plus boy lay with the Conservatives. But by the time of the 1955 election I was as far Left as I could go without joining the Communist Party; and enjoying a little letter-writing to Moscow with wonderful replies printed half in English and half in Russian. I was for the solidarity of the working-classes without yet having met the working man. There is a difference between the working man at home and the working man at work. I had an all-consuming hatred for the ways things were, and the Them and The School, and Dunking Doughnuts Clubs and all of that. And this attitude was being reinforced by the books I read. The School was, although I didn't realise it, having no positive effect on me whatsoever. What mattered were not the lessons which had to be endured, but The Rest. The Rest of the front room at home, and the open world of the juke-box caffs and the pubs, and also the books in the back cupboard of the English room. While the others were playing or organising other people's playtime I'd stay in that room culling through the books in the back cupboard. By fifteen I had worked through most of them. I liked Auden because he was easy to read, and the things he said were personal and human, and he stood committed and what he said was relevant to the world outside The School. I didn't like Isherwood as much. He seemed less active and alive, less personal and more difficult to read and much less concerned with England. I liked Orwell but thought the whole thing was a bit too laboured and deliberate—look this is the working class, see?—too much of the Socialist God and Moralist looking down on the world. Whereas Auden always seemed to be looking across. Forster I liked full stop. Virginia Woolf was hard labour. Evelyn Waugh was too stuck up. I couldn't see what people saw funny in Waugh. Spender seemed even more laboured than Orwell, and much too nice and self-conscious and inoffensive. But of all I read, Graham Greene was the most interesting. I liked the idea that stories could be written like a thriller, set in the world we lived in, and still have more, even if it was a good versus an evil (that isn't always what it seems). But *Brighton Rock* was wonderful. I admired Greene a great deal, for he seemed to have succeeded in the art of getting across to the common reader without having to talk down. I liked *Picture Post*. I've always been fascinated by this problem of getting across, or contact, two cultures that there shouldn't be, the business of communication of what one saw, felt, thought. I liked Auden, and I loved the poetry but taking part in *F6* made me realise the sad fact, that it didn't get across. The circulation was all too limited, yet Greene could be turned into a film straight out. I was for the working classes, for the underdog, for the seedy and the left behind, for the Spain that wasn't and the life that could be, and the England that seemed and still seems an impossible dream.

I was brought up in a churchgoing family, Church of England, but from early as I can remember I'd had a guilty complex about the whole thing. I preferred creeping in at the back behind the loud can't you hear me voices and standing with the parishioners who actually came from the parish, and feeling a little out of the social *it* of the place. The church appalled me by its fake and phoneyness all through with the showings off and the loud voices and the too devout to be true attitudes. Gradually I tried out the various churches around the town. The chapels were simply inhuman. They belonged to darkest Africa, the Africa that the white maiden missionary alone has seen. The Catholics seemed too immoral and too foreign. I stood at the back of the Catholic cathedral and people walked in and out, and everybody seemed to be saying something different, and either arriving or leaving and no one seemed to pay attention to what was going on in Latin. I later found that this picture of chaos and Irish whiskey isn't the general pattern of the Catholic Church in England. I felt more at home with the Anglo-Catholics. It was fun and nice and naughty, and being a rebel and no one ever turning up to the services, and full of lost ideas and so Graham Greeney it wasn't true. Loved feeling lost. The Anglo-Catholic Church seemed lost, so I joined in there. At least there were no scouts, or young people's fellowships or fashionable hats. But always there was home and the front room with its books and its rochety typewriter and the paper on which to write poems and poems and fragments.

I want to try to sum up life at home because I think it was there that I felt more keenly than elsewhere the way I was moving. At eleven I was the bright little boy who had just started on the golden ladder on which his parents never had any chance at all. The doors to the future were opened for me, the first child of working parents.

I had been brought up right. My parents had done everything they possibly could to do the right thing for their children, to provide them with the opportunities they never had, and in particular father wanted so much. They stood by the little they had, fighting against the encroachments of the buses turning round against the front door, the houses being put up in the cornfield at the back, the slow urbanisation of the area. Their guiding rules of waste not want not, work and don't waste time were passed on successfully. Their rules of try to be nice and don't be naughty failed to reach me. But in both I was terribly conscious that all their years of working and saving and stinting themselves; all the years they deprived themselves of the little pleasures of life had been for the children.

Already at fifteen I knew that I had rejected one by one the opportunities they saved up to provide me with, and I was rejecting little by little the way of life that would give me a happy and secure and better future, and for them the sense of satisfaction, and success. I was throwing dirt on home and myself. But I was also conscious that for our Dad the traditional bettering oneself would not be the success. Like The Gran's idea of The It, there was a great deal more.

I must speak proper and so I had elocution lessons, which I gave up and cultivated, to their disappointment, the accents of the scruffy and the secondary modern children. I liked the common language.

I must learn to appreciate the good cultural things, and so I had music lessons in the piano and later the violin, but these I decided I didn't want. I wanted the radio, the juke box and the hurdy gurdy of the hooligan.

I must learn that mixing with people, and with the good and right people, but not the best or top people, rather the honest and righteous people was in my own interests, that it would be good for me. I was taught how to mix and be nice. I had to learn how to grow up right and nice. I went to the church choir, and cubs, scouts, and later on for a very short time to a youth guild; and all this I left after spitting at the operators of such noble enterprises. I went to church, it was agreed; but not to the church of my parents but to some funny church with a bad reputation in a slum area where only the cranks ever went.

Slowly I poured the muck with a great show of exhibition-ism and drama on The School and the Right Way. I spurned and scorned the semi-detached world my parents had worked and saved for years to be my inheritance so that I shouldn't have to fight against all the odds as they did. I kept bad company, and I liked bad company, and I wanted to scrawl this across the ceiling of the front room at home. And I showed my dislike with as much ostentation and noise as I could.

Yet it was in the front room at home that I found the conflict within myself. First I wanted to take a back seat, to sit on the fence like a mocking bird and pull down all the sacred objects of the phoney world I saw around; to be the rebel with or without the cause; use the headmaster and all them and that place for a spittoon, shop windows as footballs; to scream out so that everybody would know—I don't like it here.

And second I wanted to build something up. There was no point and no use in merely wrecking and spitting at everything and everybody. Something had to be built up; to take a stand and show that things could be better. It was like wanting to start a railway club all over again outside the back garden: a sense of dedication, vocation, commitment, conviction, concern for The Others, The Us; all those who weren't at The School , the Lost, the ones by rejecting the semi-detached I had come to take sides with, and to stand with and by: to lead an adopted people into battle—you just sit there on the seven o'clock bus and you don't do anything. Rise up, rise up and fight, fight for more money and a better share and for life. I was possessed by a driving sense of concern and commitment and care; the battle, play my part in bringing a new England across but how to do it, who for, what about me? The People, they didn't seem to want a revolution. They seemed contented enough. I hadn't then come across the idea that unless the fervent few take the initiative then nothing will be accomplished. I hadn't yet been to work to find out that after work, physically and in every way even in a forty-four-hour week there is little energy left to work for a revolution. I hadn't then realised that when you spend twenty years working for a semi-detached and you get it, you want nothing revolutionary; just hold on tight to the bit you've got. But where was I to start, what people to join?

The Labour Party, it seemed an impossible bore. The Do-Gooders were Do-Gooders. Not only were they as phoney as the Church of England, but they seemed completely, and utterly out of contact with the world outside, pathetically so; so ignorant, as ignorant as The School of the open world of the Town.

And there was a third side: I admired Greene because he seemed able to get across, be it a story or a moral; yet Auden though he came across to me didn't reach any broader public. *Picture Post* fascinated me. There was a magazine that hadn't stooped down to the commercial undertones. It was alive, factual and got across. I wanted to find out how, in words, pictures, music to get across. I wanted to find out how to get across to the nice at The School, The People and the Fervent Few; to get across to the broadest public without having to be a servant to an intellectual discipline or a commercial tone. The whole idea of being popular while not sacrificing any of one's ideas, methods, or facts fascinated me. The School idea got across so very well, and people believed that the world was all like The School, and shouldn't change and everything was well and prospering. I wanted to write on the wall of the school in a language people would be able to read, the facts from the other side — that the world wasn't all The School, and that it was much better and more alive and interesting and vital away from The School than it was in it. And that all the things The School stood for, it was all a load of pigeon shit.

And slowly ideas and conflicts were making some sort of pattern, that began to mean something. The rebellion and rejection and opting out of the semi-detached dream upwards was searching for an alternative. I was beginning to supply reasons, coming slowly through after the rejections and the violence.

five

I WAS STILL VERY CONSCIOUS OF BEING ALONE. I DIDN'T
mind this. I wanted to be on my own. But I was conscious of
being out of it, and a feeling that I wouldn't be able to mix
even if I wanted to. There was The Arm; and the rejection of
The School and at the same time the refusal to give up going
there. The love of books and faces and places and yet however
much this egged me on, there was a nagging hatred of the
whole base and idea of The School.

At fifteen things were fusing together, and then I went into
the sixth-form and everything started moving at a much
faster pace. It was set off by the question of how was I going
to be financed if I stayed on at school. If you stay on at school
you'll have to earn enough money from somewhere to pay for
your clothes and books and pleasure and to keep yourself in
the holidays. You can't just laze around doing nothing. My
parents just couldn't do any more than keep me in the bare
essentials during term time. The paper round I had since I
was thirteen wasn't going to bring in enough to keep me. My
first idea was a job on the railway. I went down to the local
station, but they hadn't any vacancies and they didn't want
temporary workers. I then tried local firms—boot and shoe,
leather, engineering—but they too didn't want temporary
workers. After trying different approaches with different

firms it was plain that there wasn't much chance of a holiday job with enough pay to keep me at Northampton. Someone said there might be jobs on the railway over at Wellingborough or Kettering about ten miles east, and so I went over to Wellingborough to see the bloke who looked after signalling from Leicestershire right down the line to Bedfordshire. After a lot of talk and fighting and persuading, the bloke said if I came in every holiday bar Christmas he might be able to fit me in as a signal-box boy either at Wellingborough, or Kettering or Market Harborough. I remember he asked me how I thought I'd be able to get across from Northampton for six in the morning and I said I'd hitch hike. He got puzzled at this, but I think it got me the job. It must have taken him off his feet — hitching a lift to work. The job suited me fine. The money, compared with other ideas, and other people's luck, it was simply fantastic. Once I'd learnt the ropes I'd be on a basic of about six a week, and then there was overtime, and Saturday afternoons, and night work when I got a bit older. They were very hard up for staff.

The idea of working in a great big signal-box had a sense of charm about it. I'd be a key man. And that summer I started working at a signal-box in Wellingborough. The first day was awful. My hitching bravado didn't extend to the first day, and so I'd biked the ten miles across, and then dumped my bike and found the bloke who'd set me on. He asked me how I got there, and I said as I'd biked it, and he said sensible. I liked that bloke. I think he was a Yorkshireman, and he was genuine all the way through. I remember he offered me a cigarette first time I ever went to see him, when I was after the job. I liked that. The idea of being offered a cigarette by your boss. Naturally I refused: did I ... ? He never seemed like a boss. He was full of the glories of nationalisation, and the wonders of the men on the line—I'm putting you in with Wispy. You'll like Wispy. There's a lot of ill feeling among some of the men against Wispers, but I like him. I think you'll be alright with him. He's stayed on after retiring age you see—I didn't. I couldn't see how the men would go against him for that. And you'll be learning with Young Porky. He's a good Kettering lad is young Porky. Bit rough with the language, but you won't mind that. I thought of Bushland Road and The School. No I won't mind that. It struck me; this bloke knows where I've come from and yet he supposes I'll be able to take all this. Didn't treat me as being different from any of the others, but treated Me as Me, with my own personal background. They'll pull your leg hell of a lot, but Ray, you just hang on tight. He called me by my Christian name. Well, we'll go up and have a look shall we. You got your pack up—Me what?—Your sandwiches, lad—No— Well you'll have to eat at the Loco—the men'll show you where it is. Come on then. It's an important box this one. You see, all the freight comes down from Toton and the North and pulls in this yard here, and then we sort it out and send it into London. It's not a good way of getting the job done, because you see, when it gets to London it has to be half sorted out all again, but it's the best we can do till they build this new freight yard outside London. Wellingborough, it'll be a graveyard then.

I gathered later on that this bloke was an exception. He was tough as nails when he had to be. I remember watching him haul a relief signalman over the coals for some mistake he'd made that held up traffic and put men's lives in danger. But he had the reputation of being a fair man. The traffic mattered. The men mattered. The rest didn't. He was on the men's side. He worked with them, and as long as they did their job the rest didn't matter. He never interfered. He knew their jobs, and he knew where his began and ended, and he knew the traffic and the workings all through — the whole shoot right down to the last bell.

I remember going to another railway interview many years later on. I was dressed better, cleaner, tidier; and I walked into the office — you put your fag out right now, young man. It is gross bad manners to smoke in company. If you want a cigarette you ask me first — I didn't mind him telling me off for walking in with a fag in me mouth, but I didn't want the lecture. — Now I see you're an intelligent young man, and therefore I must warn you not to associate with the kind of men we have had these days, regrettable as it is , to employ in the lower grades where you'll be starting. Do not allow them to corrupt you. Stand up for yourself. Take a pride in your job, and if you have any queries or are in need of any help come to see me. Remember, my boy, promotion rests in this office and not with the Union. Don't take your problems to the other men. Bring them to me. You may have confidence in me. And then he turned to his clerk and said — I shall start this boy without a medical. We can arrange that later on. He looks fit enough. My word will be sufficient. I was glad, so glad when I went for the medical later on and failed. I then had to take it again at London, and when I went there I passed 100 per cent; and then I went back to his office to see him. It gave me great pleasure to tell him that now as he'd buggered me around I didn't want this stinking bloody job. He could have it. He told me he had never been spoken to like this by an employee in his life. I said ex-employee. He said alright, ex-employee if you will and carried on with his own lecture. I stopped him, told the bleeder straight that I hoped it'd do him good, and hoped some day someone'd put the filthy twisting bastard in his place.

No, the bloke at Wellingborough, he was straight and fair as they come. I liked him. He wouldn't say definite yes I could take the job until he had seen his superiors over the matter, but he'd do his best and then let me know. And on that first day when I was walking with him from the station to the box he told me — Ray, if you're going to let us down, will you let me know before you do, just as a personal favour. I said I would. We went into the box, and he said — Porky, here's your new lad, train him as good as you and don't teach him the bloody language first. And then — Wispy, this is Ray. And that was that. He left.

The box and the whole works seemed out of this world. Bells rang, and trains passed and Porky kept swearing down the telephone; and Wispers kept swearing at Porky and Porky would suddenly jump up and swing a lever across and jump back on to his stool, and pick up another telephone and yell into that, laughing and swearing. I found out later that the whole exhibition was part of Porky's drama, to prove to me that the job was a good one, and he knew his job and he was a top rate key man. There was a great pride in the job. Before I was shown any kindness or before I was asked any questions, they had to prove to me that the job was not for the stupid or the lazy. Until they had impressed me with the importance of the job, I was not going to be any more than a half-acknowledged observer. Very slowly I learned the mysteries of the two telephones, and the two switchboards, and the bell codes and the three books that had to be kept up to date. Porky would explain to an irate control panel at Leicester how it was the new lad. The train movements we made were reported to the regional traffic control centre at Leicester. I remember vividly one control bloke called Alun — Porky I tell you, you want to kill that bloody new lad will you — he's fooking menace — sent the bloody Derby, tells every bugger it's for Nottingham ... That was my greatest fear, directing trains the wrong way. It was all very easy to do. There was a junction a few miles away where the Derby road branched from the Nottingham road. The signalman at the junction relied on bell signals and phone calls to tell him which way to route a train. Usually it was simple as the traffic followed a plan which every signalman knew, but there were extras, and lates, and non-timetabled traffic. I remember once when I was on my own getting the whole thing mixed up. The control at Leicester told me by phone that the first of two trains was for Nottingham road, and the second for Derby. They were both iron ore specials. I got the message mixed up, and it wasn't discovered till the trains had taken the wrong road, and that I had made a mistake. Leicester, the central control would tell us, and that would be me and I'd tell Wisp the signalman so he could fix the bell signals, and then I'd phone to the junction box. We were a sort of regional control, a middle man, and we sorted the traffic out for the boxes up the line where the junctions were. The job was very important. There had to be absolute trust in other people's messages by bell code or phone. If one wasn't accurate, mistakes could easily be made. I grew to like the voice of Alun from Leicester control. He became one of my best railway friends, but we never met. We were just voices on the phones. It was funny — at sixteen, Leicester for me was this strange gruff voice down the phone line, and I imagined Alun sitting at some office in the main street looking down on the bright lights of the big city. I never imagined the control could be anywhere near the actual railway line; and I've still to find out where it really is. But after two weeks training on a 9 to 5 basis and though still amazed at the speed and skill of Porky, the Bloke visited us.

You'll be on your own next week. Start six to two. Porky you go back to Kettering; and Wispy you look after our lad next week. And that was it. The training was finished. I was in.

The first week was hell. Wispers sweated blood putting my mistakes right, but by the time I was ready to go back to The School and the sixth-form I was alright. I knew the trains and I knew my traffic. I knew my way around the complicated switchboards and telephones. I became Our College Lad, and I liked that. And the hitch-hiking only rarely failed to bring me on shift in time, coming down the hill in a baker's van every morning for six when I was on earlies. It dazzled the men, and it shook me, how I did it: hitch-hiked to work every morning.

In that summer holiday I had taken the first steps in growing up. I had learnt more, I felt, in that box than the sixth-form would be able to teach me in what concerned me and interested me most.

There was Wispy, most of all Wispy. He was sixty-seven, and two years over retiring age. This meant that some of the younger men who had hoped for his job when he retired were being done down out of the key job, and it *was* the key job, full of prestige, but with only a few shillings more in pay. The thwarted ones, they tried every method they knew to unseat the Wisp: in the Union, with the Inspectors, making his life far more tough than it could possibly have been otherwise, and it was tough enough without the age factor, let alone the antagonism of some of the fellow workers. Yet he stuck it out. He needed the money. Wispy, people said, was a Communist. But to me, he was the first man I ever met who was in all sincerity and honesty for the workers and of the workers. He was a big bloke in the Trade Union and Labour. He would bring his literature from the *Soviet Weekly* to *Tribune* to work with him. The men, even his enemies, would bring their Union dues and their Union troubles to him. He was for strikes over wages. He was out for large differentials in the signalling grades. It was the time when A.S.L.E.F., the locomen's union, came out on strike to support the claim of top money for top men. Wispy wanted the signalmen to do the same. They were just as much key men as the loco lads. There was a great gulf at the time between the locomen and the running staff. Even Wisp was affected by it. Spitting at the Locos and cursing the key men, but the whole affair and the rivalry were more out of jealousy than anything else. Wispers had got an enormous admiration for the guts of the locomen in sticking to their guns right through to the withdrawal of labour.

Wispy said — nationalisation, it's made it worse lad. Before we had bosses. Now you don't know who your bosses are, and they does you down just the same. How can you have nationalisation in capitalist society? He explained the wages structure to me. Wages structures and rates — it's a fascinating business, like working out how much a type page of 440 words is going to bring you in. It was the lessons from him that drew me more than anything into taking Economics as a third for the sixth-form course. It took, and it still does, years as an ordinary signalman, and then as a relief signalman working in boxes when the regular man took sick, or there was a vacancy waiting to be filled, and then the years of waiting for the man at the key box, the man like Wispers to die or retire. If you made one mistake, you were downgraded right back to porter at times. It was a lonely job, needing a great amount of personal discipline. Decisions had to be taken alone. The only contact was the telephone and the bell signals, and there wasn't always time for these to be checked on. One mistake and your fellow signalman down the line could be led into making a mistake, or one mistake yourself and mistakes meant lives, human beings. You had to have the complete confidence of the other men in the line. It took nearly thirty years of hard graft to even join the waiting list for a key job like Wispers's, and if there was any blemish on your record the chances were very slim. The chance of a clean record was about equal to that of a lorry driver. And what did the key job entail — easy shifts, good money, and an end to the hard graft? No, the shifts were the same as everyone else's, the graft was twice as hard. It was the busiest box on the line for twenty miles either way. And the reward—I think it was eight shillings a week more than a relief signalman's, and overtime in the key boxes was prohibited. Why then the waiting list? The railwayman's pride is something that goes very deep. Wispers's job was THE key job in the district, the highest achievement, the greatest responsibility, the highest point a signalman in the district could reach, and with it went the greatest prestige. I have an enormous admiration for railwaymen. It's a job, particularly a signalman's in the older boxes, carrying enormous responsibility. The mental strain is fantastic, and with it goes a physical strain equal at times to that of a coalface worker; but unlike the face worker the danger to yourself is far outweighed by the danger that in your mistakes the innocent, the unknowing, the general public can be hurt. I still think, and particularly with these key jobs, the pay is ridiculously low, ridiculously low.

He'd ask me which 'side' I'd be on if there was a war. Wispers'll stand with the Russians. Him and the railway were the first contact of any depth I had with the old world divisions, the solidarity of the working classes, rich and poor, workers and bosses, and the greatness of the Labour Movement. But Wispy was an exception. He was an individualist, in many ways an intellectual. When I was sixty, he said, I thought about religion and I turned Catholic. It was weeks before I found out that this was true. It's a wonderful religion. It's wonderful, Catholic. At sixty he became a Roman Catholic convert, from nothing. He was married, and on some afternoons when he had forgotten his pack-up we would see his wife as she came down to the box with his forgotten lunch. And he had a woman. Lovely gal. I went to see the Fathers, and I said is it wrong because she's so beautiful and such a lovely young body on her. I love her. I can't see no wrong in it. I still love the missus. Wispy, he accommodated a love of the work, the men, the Church, the Labour, the Union, a wife, an only child, a woman, and there was nothing incongruous. Working alone with a man in a box that grew smaller each time I turned up for the eight-hour stint, you learn a great deal about your partner. You learn to be tolerant. It's rather like sharing a flat, like living together. There are the two of you, and between the two of you, you have to hold the fort over the main lines, the two freight yards, the loco shed, making your mashings and looking across at the red fires from the iron blast furnaces on the other side of the lines. The two of you have to find a level of communication. For me it was Auden and all that, in technicolour. For me it was romantic, a little; and yet it was too hard, too real. But I think it was the romance and the pride in being on the railway that kept me in the job, through the holidays.

There was lobbing your phlegm out of the sliding windows, stoking up the black grate, polishing the fender, learning how to roll cigarettes. And Wisp was a romantic, nostalgic over the passing of the old working-class world. He'd give me little lectures. When you're sixty you want to be able to think back to these days, and say thank God it aint like this now. He had the pride in the job, and the belief in the solidarity of the workers, and the hope that one day the exploitations and the hardship would end. It doesn't matter, he'd tell me, if the pride and the solidarity go to make way for decent money and conditions. It'll be a sacrifice well made. It'll be up to the likes of you to build up a pride in other things, better things.

In my first summer at work I had found where I felt and thought my feet belonged. I liked Wispy. He had a few strands of white hair, just a little and he would comb it continuously. He loved himself, and knew he had the charm and the looks and a proud dignity. On sunny afternoons he'd put his hand in his leather belt, stand by the window that faced the road bridge, his lips puckered, sucking and chewing at the end of the rolled cigarette, spitting from time to time, and looking at the girls on the bikes, with their dresses being blown around by the wind, as they crossed the bridge.

Then I went back to Northampton for the last time that summer, and back to The School and the sixth-form. Things had started to move, the way I wanted it and liked it.

six

ONE SWING AWAY FROM THE SEMI-DETACHED I FEEL I should explain, I want to go into more fully. At the time it was very important. As I've said I moved away before I was fifteen and before I reached the sixth-form from the Church of England to the Anglo-Catholics. In my first year of the sixth-form I decided that the Anglo-Catholics and the business of going to the Anglos because it seemed the Church of the lost souls wasn't really satisfactory. It was cranky and eccentric and done to a large extent for effect; as another of my look at me the rebel, the one who doesn't like The School tags. And so I went into the front room and took out the books on religion, and pieces of paper from all over and sat down and thought and read and wrote and read about religion, and God and the Church. Trying to work out lines of definition is rather like trying to formulate a party policy for a party that has questioned and found wanting some, if not all, of the tenets it grew up with. I thought about where I stood, and what I was going to do about it if I believed. I started at the beginning. I believed in God, the Christian God. There were from that fact whole chunks I had grave doubts about, but I had doubts about so many things. I had to put the doubts aside, and be positive and take any steps of faith that were necessary or I would remain a cranky lover of lost souls and incense swinging, and I wasn't going to be that. I finished up by coming to the conclusion that I believed in the Catholic Church. There are a lot of pointers that may have helped me along to that—Wispers, Graham Greene, parents, school— but as far as I could, I went about this cold-bloodedly and coolly. It was an intellectual thing—I believed in the Roman Catholic Church.

I made up my mind that before I did anything about taking physical steps to become a Roman Catholic I would spend a whole half term at a monastery somewhere. I wanted somewhere quiet, on the Catholic side and away from people. I found one near Coalville in Leicestershire and I booked in for a free four days. I remember travelling up by bus through Leicester which seemed so big and ugly and northern, to Coalville; and there I saw my first coalmine. I had always imagined coalmines to be in deep northern or Welsh valleys, and all black and dirty, but there were no romantic black faces at Coalville. It was just like a factory. It didn't hit me that there were pit-head baths for months after I'd gone away. The mine seemed like the railways, full of solidarity and romance and pride and dignity, all in the very best sense.

But I was going to the monastery and I did little more than pass through Coalville. I went to the monastery and came away four days later my mind made up—I was going to be Catholic, but I had lost my 'religion'. I wasn't going to be a priest or a monk or anything in the way of a professional religious. I remember walking down a hill towards Leicester and seeing Leicester all smoke and mist and grime and chimneys below, and thinking; well now another step towards a definition, of my own place, of me, of what to do and where

I belonged. I belonged down there. It was like a statement of belief. If anyone had told me that in two, three years' time this would be literally true I wouldn't have believed them.

I remember I hadn't any money, so I had to hitch a lift through Leicester back into Northampton. Funny thing this is: from as long back as I can remember money hasn't stopped me. I wouldn't be surprised by feeling in my pockets and finding no money and being 10, 100, 300 miles away from the next bit of money. I'd walk, or hitch or jump a train if I knew the line. Well, after a long course of instruction I was received into the Roman Catholic Church on a Christmas Eve. Within six months the mist around my definition papers had cleared. I was R.C. full stop. It has been like that ever since.

What sort of Catholic am I? I think that's my affair. It's as disrespectful to ask a person what sort of Catholic he is, as asking him what sort of lover he is. I may write about myself. I may 'expose' thoughts, actions, feelings, responses, but actual categorical definition for me ends at Religion R.C.: Sex. M. I have read that Graham Greene is a bad Catholic, and I have heard that Cindy's no bloody good in bed. I don't know. I'm not interested. Only God can know about Graham Greene just as only Cindy's lover can know about Cindy. These are things that are between two people exclusively, beyond the line of communication, outside any public area.

The trip to the monastery, and my becoming a Catholic gave clearer definition to two pointers in the eternal question —what do I do with this life? I had solved the question before I had any idea of methods, of how to put the answer into facts. I was going to take a stand. I was going to do something with ME. Marriage, getting on, security, etc, etc, were second to the desire to do something, to create something. I'd got two pointers. I belonged down there, with the people. The second was that I knew that if I was going to be able to retain any sense of perspective, any sense of consciousness I must have the front room, the books, paper, the libraries, museums, monasteries — the time to think and brood; the times of going underground.

My becoming a Catholic was my first very conscious act. I had always been conscious of taking decisions before, that would affect the future; but this was the first thing I ever did where I went into the moves coldly, methodically, analytically; and then took the necessary steps. There was nothing emotional in my change of religion. It was a simple intellectual step taken with thought, thought coming from the question where on religion do I stand, if at all, what do I believe.

I've dug up a screed I wrote on the night after I came back. I want to put it in just as it came then. It may help you to see the point better than any looking back I could do.

Life leaves a man with very little time for consideration of his actions. Prompted by this genuine desire for time to consider my life, I made a pilgrimage to Mount Saint Bernard Abbey. On Friday, 13 July 1956, I hitch-hiked to Coalville to examine my past, present and future life in relationship to God and Man.

On my arrival I found everything as I had expected — smiling monks — bells — Mass — simplicity. I was struck by the simplicity of the Church. There were no statues of saints; no stained-glass windows to stand between myself and

God. Nothing but bare stone walls and marble floors focused on to the Cross and Tabernacle. I felt for the first time in my life, very happy, at peace and completely at home.

On Saturday morning after Mass I examined my past and found there an amazing sequence of events reaching their climax in my present visit to the monastery. My constant striving to be at peace with God and my ardent desire to help mankind were the two major factors in my past. My past was finalised now but these two factors were to me as far apart as God and the devil. After dinner Fr. R. spoke about his experiences in China. I felt at once a deep desire to help China, the Chinese and Man. During the afternoon I toured the Abbey and was impressed by the holy jokes told by the Fr. If only the world would listen to holy jokes they would really laugh, not just smile at smut. I spoke to Fr. B. after tea about my past life and the sequence of events. Fr. spoke on union with God but this union appeared to cancel out my love of mankind. I read at Fr's. request 'This Tremendous Lover' by Eugene Boylan and found some very useful advice but again could not unite my love of Man with Union with God. I prayed — thought — slept ... On Sunday after High Mass, I saw Fr. B. and discussed effective prayer and my conflict between God and Man. I was still mystified. We considered my future and came to the rational conclusion that I had no vocation for any form of organised religious life but that I had a vocation for a special and unusual type of work which God would make clear in time.

Later, Fr. R. blessed my Rosary which will be said with the intention of the conversion of sinners and as a reparation for the harm done to God by my own sin. In the afternoon I walked up to the Calvary. From the top I could see a group of teenagers smoking and mocking a figure of Christ. This was England — These people who did not care about God. These were the people who did not care about Communism either. This was England — couldn't care less. I walked down to the church and prayed as I never have prayed before.

I saw Fr. B. again after tea and talked about my vocation. We came to the conclusion that it was probably apostolic and may be literary. He lent me two books including 'One with Jesus' by De Jaegar, SJ. That evening, Sunday, 15 July 1956, I said my prayers and got into bed. I opened the book and took notes up to page 12. I read that page and noticed an NB marking in the margin. I had to re-read it because I just could not understand it. Then it suddenly hit me. 'I wish in you, and by you to live as it were a second life wholly of love, which will be the complement and continuation of my earthly life at Nazareth and in Palestine.'

I could read no more — I was happy — I had found an answer to all my problems. I had found my past, present and future. Why did I pray when I saw those teenagers mocking Christ? Why do I want to act the Sorrowful mysteries of the Rosary? Why did I want to hold out my arms during the Canon of the Mass? Why do I pray and feel the way I do towards Man? I had discovered my life — my reality — my past — my present — my future — The fact that Christ is in me. The fact that He now wants me to be united with Him in His work now means that union with God is also union with Man.

Mass on Monday morning meant more to me that it has ever meant to me, but today is Monday — the day I face the world again. The sadness that comes with this fact is overwhelming and has to be faced. The pieces of my life have fitted together as well as a jigsaw puzzle when completed. I arrived on Friday like the pieces all mixed up in a box. I leave on Monday in one flat picture but that picture has not been glued and I am afraid that portions of it may fall out in my journey back to the world. It will need all God's glue to keep the puzzle of me intact. I made only one real resolution — 'One with Jesus' — but Fr. B. came to see me for the last time and a number of immediate resolutions were made.

I had tea and left quickly and quietly the monks and the peace of the monastery. I walked on to the Leicester road and came to a hill of bare and rugged rock. From here I looked back at the monastery and the Calvary which overhung it. I turned and faced a fog. Slag heaps replace the monastery. Tall chimneys belched smoke in an effort to replace the Calvary. I felt a desire to bring the monastery into the Leicester smog. I know now I have a job to do. I know that somehow I must help to bring the monastery into the world — I know now as I have never known before — I have a chance to become the monastery or the world, sinner or saint, I believe I will never have this chance again. I left the Abbey grounds at 4 and by 6.30 p.m. I had hitch-hiked into Northampton for 7d. a wet coat, a wet head and a happy soul...

seven

NORTHAMPTON — THIS PLACE — MY FIRST TASTE OF
the great down there, the land beyond the slag heaps —
Northampton — found my first cigarettes here, lying in a
packet of twenty Woodbine in the middle of the road, all
eight of them, just lying there on the pavement. And smoking
became a part of things. In the four days at the monastery I
smoked more than in any eight on the railway. Smoking
became a part of things.

And then the first taste of beer — half a glass of bitter at a
little bar on Regent Square. The pub's still there. Haven't
been in it for years. I didn't like the stuff. Took to bottles, and
then black and tan, scrumpy, black velvets; and then at last to
the big watery pints and pints of Midland bitter. Gin in
London. A settling down at whisky.

But going down there started it off, with me on my own
moving through the bars the Yanks used. The big bar, it's a
fishing tackle shop now, but in those days it was the big Yank
bar, just on the fringe of the Town. It was cheap. There were
always people ready to buy me drinks — negroes, white girls.
There was a large German juke box in the corner and Aspro
and peanut machines along the walls, and almost every night
the bar'd get filled right up to the ceiling with the white girls
and the American negroes and the visits from the base MPs,

and the Town lads and the inevitable fight with the glasses
going against the walls and heads going against the Aspro
machines. And there would always be the lonely ones — the
girl from Huddersfield working her way south towards
London, the kid from Dublin or Belfast and the Cockneys
and the Northerners waiting like me to get the feel of the
place before moving into the Town. Very slowly I moved in,
and from the Yanks bar to the Town proper; to large rooms
with a juke box and a skittle table — bars where whites took
over and the negro was the odd man out.

Down at the GG's the night Little Tony had the big fight
and there was blood all the way down the road to the bus
station, and there was this glass eye rolling about in the
gutter, and this cut up kid wandering around with blood all
over his face and his coat torn in two looking for his lost glass
eye. The way when a fight started all the girls would go back
to the wall and wait for the end, and then help to clear everybody up and away before the police turned up. And then
when the pubs had finished we'd go down to one of the Cyp
caffs* on Bridge Street for the late night egg and chips, and
clearing out before the gaffer came along with the bill. Funny
thing about Northampton, after the pubs shut you go and
have a meal. Most other places you go for black coffee or coke
or something, but in Northampton you go have a meal. And
then the taxis home, and the parties and the singing and the
being drunk and putting it on for this welfare woman who
wanted to find out about how young people lived and why as
if she hadn't got eyes in her head; everybody inventing names

---

* run by Greek-Cypriots.

and telling stories, and she took it all down, and believed every bloody little bit. Then the Sunday afternoons down at the Hollow Caff, or the place that's now an Indian eating house, just sitting and shouting out of the window down to the street, just sitting and talking all afternoon over one cup of tea; and then Sunday night at the pictures. When Bill Haley's *Rock Around the Clock* got shown, and the first Elvis and the way Tommy Steele was all soft and stupid almost from the second disc he cut. It was the start of something. Everyone felt this — with the James Dean pictures, and the start of the teenage thing. It was like the start of a revolution; coming in with the big noise right at the beginning of the whole thing.

And all the time, all through this there was The School. But it was only like a job. I worked at Lyons down in London, and then came back and worked at The School, and then there was nights at the Post Office; and the weekends away down in London, and coming back from The Smoke on a Sunday night from Euston and getting in with the milkman on a Monday morning and changing uniforms and being ashamed of the change, and then straight off into The School like all I wanted to do was go to sleep and sleep. It was just like working in a factory. Sitting down and keeping your trap shut, and looking at your watch all the time, waiting for the hands to move round, the bell to ring just like it was the hooter at the factory. Outside, up the jitty** and cover up all the things people might see that showed you belonged to that place, and with the tie in the pocket taking a slow smoke up

---

*   Lyons tea-rooms.

**   an alleyway.

the jitty, clipping to cross the road into the caff, a cup of tea, a couple of records and making up my mind — what to do for the night-away or The Town or the front room.

One half term I said I wanted to leave. They said alright. I left. Had no idea what I was going to do. I just wanted to get out of that place. But before the half term was over I went down on my hands and knees, let me come back, please let me come back, I'll be a good little boy, honest I will, give us just one more chance will you. I went back. There were only two compensations about that place, the rest of it stank; like a sewer only it pretended that the sewer was a pie in the sky which if you played the game their way would be yours. No, not for me. I'd seen something I liked, like the start of a revolution that worked and meant something and didn't drag you down or push you up over the others; and this was It. The movement back completed a life, a way of living that worked — primary passions, primary colours.

You see, what were at eleven for me the scruffy secondary moderns had become what they are — The Goods, and the They changed to We, and their way of life to Our Way of Life — back to Grandfather, back to Him, back to East Street, back to the point where our Dad had to get off to find Bushland Road and security; back there to start again and let the light in, find a dignity and a life to make the most of without having to get out — a way of life, a whole culture.

I had the front room, the signal-box, The School, but beneath it and above it all there was this way of life and what was scruffy became dignity, and what was naughty became a way of life, a positive; and what was nice became fake, the cultural tag-ons that went with houses like Bushland Road.

The outfit I'd bought; the trousers were black and tight and the jacket was straight blue and draped, the way I did my hair, the way you wore your face it wasn't a rebellion any more, it wasn't being naughty, it wasn't any longer a reaction against the nice and phoneyness of The School. It was my life, the only way of life I knew, the primary, basic and best; the ground to keep my feet on no matter what I did with the rest of me. My feet were staying on the ground and on the ground with a dignity and pride and a whole new future where people were people before they were anything else — that's what you taught me — the first town, the first time I found the ground and knew it for what it was — the goods, the genuine, the most honest and straight and most open of all. It was the goods, the genuine, the primary — and it mustn't get spoiled by being made nasty and wicked and sinful and evil and wrong; nor must it be taken over by Bushland Road into something nice and laughed at behind closed curtains. The infinite depths of the Establishment bog wasn't going to suck this one under. That's what you taught me. So that where there should have been a proud arrogance there was only the aggressive and a hate that was almost unendurable, a hate for you, and The School, and all the lies and niceness you stood by and for.

But there were compensations — one man, a few friends — a teacher who taught that Shakespeare was as important and vital and wonderful as Auden and all that, because what he had to say about the human condition, about life wasn't a tale of an Italian aristocrat of the fifteenth century but the stuff beneath the costume. It was — all human life is here, the whole of life — with the *News of the World* story thrown in for the interest, to keep the story going. It wasn't that I admired him. It wasn't the person who taught that mattered but the way it came across. This was important. He made for me the whole of language come alive, and the whole of literature vital — the social scene, the human scene, the temporal conflicts, the eternal struggles. The whole thing came home and alive. English language, art, literature, words — the attempts at getting facts across, information, what it feels like, what it felt like, what it was, what it is to be a human being, to have been born. For him the whole thing ran through from Langland through to the Organ Grinders' journal, the latest Fabian pamphlet and the *Sunday Express* serial. It all mattered. It was all in.

But, and there was a big But. The books were in the package deal with The School and the way up, on to the best possible University, and on to the best possible outlet in teaching or commerce, or what have you. We were the one in 130 of our age group. We were the top of the cream. They could talk about the ones who missed the message and went in for Beatnik, or Brewery, or Drifting, or Nothing; the ones who wouldn't or couldn't keep climbing, as failures, not just of the system but failures for themselves. They hadn't done themselves justice. We were the select who could appreciate and make judgements and it was a sin unto ourselves if we abandoned being the select, the upper intelligentsia. No, that was the big But, the one part I couldn't stomach. There were other things; things like on the Town, on the Railway, in London, things that went on that were part of something else,

---

* William Langland (1332–1400) author of *Piers Plowman*.

another way of life just as valid — No, not just as valid — they were the goods; the life, the generous instinct. The one in 130 were not just select, superior; they were not for a closed circuit look at better things. They weren't and shouldn't have been superior, nor cut off in the closed circuit of the best appreciation. For me the whole love of words and language and accents one man gave me, it was something I liked, and I am grateful. It was something I specialised in, and I couldn't and can't see how that makes it in any way superior, or better, or that I can appreciate life or art any more fully than anyone who hasn't specialised in this use of words, language. No, I go my way, and my way is mine and I stay where I belong, on the ground.

There was one other compensation in a group of people, the same age, a group that got the tags from the rest as being Pansy, Religious, — the arty farties, the Grubbies, the Grundies. Bright in varying degrees and varying intellectual ways, most of them came from the back streets, sometimes a generation removed but originally from the blocks of streets, and were conscious of this and in different degrees, proud of it. This made them rather wonderful in a school where most of the kids went through the School's biological processing completely unconscious and unconcerned of either what was happening outside the School, or of what was happening to them inside. This was almost the only group conscious of what was happening to them through being at that place.

There was a consciousness of the old, the back streets, the old gels, and generations before us that moved from the villages into the town; and the language of the old, and the stories from the old world. And a consciousness of the new, the whole new thing that was coming through James Dean and money and Elvis and Steele and how the world of the back streets was breaking up and this new was coming through, superimposed on top of the old. To me the new was something so great, so wonderful, something that one just had to be part of. For many of the others it was an attack on both the old they knew as kids, and the learning and higher things they were only just beginning to acquire. But more important than the consciousness of what was going on outside, was the consciousness of what was happening to us, of our own position. For all of us The School was the unifying theme, the one thing one hated so much and so deeply. The weekly sixth-form exclusive with the headmaster where the blurb was handed out and pushed across so appealing, so subtly, and so the tradition of The School goes on.

And as everyone parted so I went to Leicester, and that was the final end of Northampton as being a home. The roots had by then been torn up. I'm glad they got torn up. I don't want to put them down in this town again. But I'm glad for being born here. I'm glad I went away. Glad I went the way I did. I want to travel on, seeking and looking at discarded roots, for threads, sparks that are still alive; piecing them together and doing my best to get through with some picture of this ME.

I suppose the threads that are still alive from this place are our Pop Jimmy Gosling, English, Geography, the front room, the first Town I ever went in, the Grundies — and the rest is just a memory. People I loved. Things I hated. A town of the past. The place I was born in. A c/o address for all my mail. I want to move on, through other memories, from place to place, face to face on through to other memories of what seem to me to have been the swing, searching years; the years when I began to find out where I wanted to stand, and what I wanted to do. Once I'd found the ground, we have to build, all of us, build—the ground, it's too valuable to leave fallow—build, build, but how? Wander, wander over the ground and find the best lines for the foundation; sink charges in case of oil or gold beneath the surface; find that first and quickly and then build—I mean this, this it's the only one I know I've got. I want the full effect. I want the present. Please, let me make the most of it.

.   .   .

In Northampton, there's this statue, the only one there is in the centre. It's to an M.P. the borough sent back four times in defiance of the constitution; M.P. for Northampton from 1880 to 1891. A man called Charles Bradlaugh. It's got some wonderful words round it, and no one ever reads them—always liked this—it's good, so good.

> *Electors of Northampton, work!*
> *The day will soon be here,*
> *When you will have to give your votes*
> *And give them without fear;*
> *For freedom's battle ne'er was won*
> *By cowards in the past,*
> *Nor can it be sustained*
> *By men who fear the blast.*
> *Then toil, men, toil in freedom's cause,*
> *Rest not content with vain applause,*

Humanity needs better laws
To win these we'll send Bradlaugh!
'Tis not to rob rich lords of lands,
Oppress as they would you,
Nor property make insecure,
To feed a lawless few;
But to make way for those to rise,
Who hard yet humbly toil,
And give to all some interest
In Nature's gift, the soil.

You move from anecdote to anecdote. You have your story to tell, but after each going away, after each anecdote you have returned to this place. You have always come back.

True. I can't deny it. I shouldn't want to. If I came back now it would be for physical reasons; money; because I had to. But before when I came back I rejected one more of the beliefs and dashed one more of the hopes my home and parents held in me. That is why I have put in the anecdote on anecdote, to show how I shed the skins I was born with until I found a shape I could come to terms with. But my parents never stood in my way. It was my life. That was a great fundamental family belief. It's your own life. It was more important even than growing up right, and being nice; this belief in individual freedom. They felt deeply and let me go my way.

Haven't you been cruel?

Maybe. But I can find no hope and no future in the niceness and rightness I was brought up to revere, and told to work my way into. Whatever the cost I have to go on. The rejection of the nice and right way up is, I feel, complete. I have closed all doors to a future that promised to be better than others, the way up and above. The ways to anything higher I have closed. I have my fields of specialisation and narrow-trimmed activity, but it rests on a common, popular, general, the average, and there is the future. From the common, the ground inwards to myself and not outwards or upwards.

Do you regret any of this?

No. None at all. I want to get out of this place. I have told the story. I have given examples to show how, and why I left behind the right way up that was, or should have been within the reach of my capabilities. When I stop all this travelling I shall take out these notes, and shall take from them what I need for my next moves.

You treat life like a game of chess.

Maybe. I could draw a diagram for you, to give what I see as the progression towards my present position. It might interest you. It might have been a far better method of getting across to you the points I have made by using examples and anecdotes. It might have been better. But you do see that this is the past. Looking back I can see it like a game of chess, so many moves to what is really important, vital and to me the essence of life — the now, immediate, the present — and that isn't a game of chess. The past wasn't either. It only looks that way, looking back. It wasn't then. I must go.

There are no trains now. It is too late.

It doesn't worry me. How late?

You can still take a meal in the town, if you hurry.

If I take a meal I shall want to be alone. I do not want to tell you everything. The distant past is, I find, comparatively easy to look back on now. But I have other memories. I have the present to brood over. I don't want you to hear everything. I do not want everything to go into this.

There is nothing I can do to help you, then?

Nothing.

Your mind is still made up. You won't stay.

Not now. If I come back and stay I won't inform you.

All that is left then, is good night?

You don't wish me luck?

Alright — good luck — good night.

Good night. Look. I was coming out of London once up the A5 with a Jewish friend. We were in a Jaguar. We came through Dunstable and were doing around eighty on the other side through the chalk cutting. Suddenly we saw this pile-up in front with the police cars and the ambulance. We put on the brakes and we stopped. I didn't go out to have a look, but my friend did. He came back and slumped in the seat, and he said: "Anda Jesus Vept!" There was a sigh. "I say you haven't got a cigarette have you?" It was one dead, one dying, one injured, and one scot-free. I was tired, very tired. It wasn't the dead or the dying or the injured that had my sympathy. It was the scot-free.

Why did you tell me that?

Doesn't matter. Good night.

eight

I DON'T WANT TO KNOW ANY MORE ABOUT THIS TOWN.
I have the picture. I've taken the meal. I have the message. I'm
not going home. I aint going to ring that front door bell. I
have seen the writing on the wall, and taken note. This town
don't love you no more. Pompous fool—that he should
believe it ever loved him, that it ever even knew him. Liar,
liar, liar, pornographer, pornographer, scandal monger. There
are things that are better left unsaid. True. Quote.

I'll move north. Hitch a truck ride. Sit in the cab of a BRS*
going up the old A5. Odd villages, townships, dots just like
they are on the topographical map. Dawn. Not yet.
Coalminers off to work on bicycles. Dots just like they are on
the population maps. We pull across the asphalt of a juke
box never closed caff. The driver, said he was a poet in his
spare time. Showed me some of his poetry. Alright. I like
lorry drivers. It isn't like driving a train. There is less responsibility, more freedom. British roads don't have rails; they're
just a little bent in parts.

"You wouldn't believe it. I tell you la. You wanna come in
this caff bout nine, ten, eleven o'clock at night. There's these
kids. Kids from all over. Walsall, Brum, Leicester,

---

* British Road Services.

Nottingham. All over the place they come from. Come out here on their motor-bikes. They come in the caff and start selling themselves to all these geezers who come from all over. Some of the lorry drivers too. They sit in this caff, and wait to get picked up; and then out in the fields in the car with the geezer, and then back here and all over again. One of 'em were telling me other night. About ten bob a time. Reckons on making a fiver a night. There's only young lads. Sixteen. Seventeen. Selling themselves. I've come in here, seen near forty on 'em. Doing a right roaring trade. Makes you bleeding wonder don't it. Cup of tea, lad?"

"I'll pay."

"You won't. You sit down lad. I got the easy job. Driving. You got nowt to do."

Walk to the juke box. It's battered with footmarks all around the protective bottom. Touch it. It rattles. Put a shilling in. Press; whirl. Lights. Music. Words. Love. At Last. That voice on the record. Holding that mug of tea in my hand. A cigarette. The face in the tea leaves at the bottom of the mug. Keep moving. On, on, on. Dawn. Morning. Birkenhead. Blue buses. Through the Mersey Tunnel. St. George's Square. City of Liverpool.

"See you again some day?"

"Keep smiling."

Keep moving on, and on. No full stops. Only semi-colons. Please.

. . .

What am I trying to do, in this book I mean? Write an autobiography, some documented description of what I have done? No I don't want to do this. I don't want this to be fact as fact. It isn't. It's only based on fact. I don't want it to be autobiography. Yes, yes, it's personal, self-centred. I want it that way. I think that's the best way I can get across. Get across what? The moves and wandering of the Me towards some point of definition, some lines of discipline, some way of living.

And now I think I've reached the stage where I move from a negative look at qualities and ideas I've thrown away towards the positive — the ideas, hereditary and unconsciously accumulated that I have retained, and those I have more recently acquired, more consciously gone out of my way to make my own.

Through the sifting of the attitudes and ideas I didn't choose myself, only two have come through relatively unscathed. The first of these is the front room, the monastery, books, paper, wanting to shut myself up alone and hammer out, get into concrete some idea, or thought, or buzz.

And the second is the determination to be in contact, to keep on the ground level a half to cock mirror (self-centred, personal) and to move this across faces and places in an England that I feel a part of as if the very chalk of the cliffs were a part of my bones, and particularly this part of the country, north of Bletchley, where the ironstone merges into the coal measures; and a sense of movement — of an England that changes so wonderfully from city to city, a series of dense urban blots on an England that I have never quite understood, an England as a part of Britain, an England of peace and quiet, and stability—no that's not my England. The England I know, and the England I love is an England of constant change and constant movement of peoples, a proud arrogant mongrel race intense and stubborn but with this wonderful sense of movement.

But I wasn't brought up to this. I had to rediscover my own heritage, and doing so I had to cut out most of the terribly British things I'd been brought up in. And doing this with a hate and an aggressiveness meant that the picture in the mirror of my England wasn't quite true, even to myself. The aggression and the hate came in — to be able to say, look you British bastards this land isn't a land of red pillar-boxes and straight faces, it's a living land, a land of violence and passion and change.

I went to Liverpool in 1957–58, and I put down my responses. While I was at Leicester I taped this and played them over to a great friend. He listened to them.

What do you think?

It's alright, but things aren't like that any more. It's alright, this seedy nasty; this the bad old times with a touch of nostalgia and drama thrown in; but it isn't the present. But look, this is Leicester; up there, Liverpool, it is like that, things haven't changed as they have down here. They haven't the chances, the great boom that this part of England has.

Alright, look, even if things are like that in Liverpool. Why go out of your way to paint them in the way only a twisted man could be proud of? Why do you have to harp on them? Look, ever since I've known you, you've had this flair for the seedy, for the criminal fringe, for looking at the things for the bad side, seeing things all the time as good and bad and then saying but because the bad is alive and the good is dead, then the bad is so much better. Like an anti-romantic, you've got this letch for looking out for the seedy and the nasty and the old, as if you enjoyed this, and enjoyed rubbing this into the faces of all the people you hate.

Well I do, that's why I want it that way, to rub it in their faces.

That won't do. It won't do at all.

It's taken a long while to stop looking for the decay, a long while to be able to watch a back street block pulled down and be able to say—there it goes. I knew it. It's a pity, in a way; but the chances, don't let's miss the chances for the change. A long while for the aggression and the hate to become a positive so that I hate you because of what you have done becomes I hate you and all you stand for because of what you stand in the way of: for the seedy and the decay to go, and go without becoming nice and dead, without losing the spontaneity and the life: to move from the Teddy Boy to the Teenage Thing without selling out a birthright and a generous impulse: to move from an aggression to an arrogance, a pride in a way of life: for the negative to become a positive.

And so I took out a folder marked Liverpool and I made up my mind that they were going in, here, as the picture in the mirror, as the way it looked when I first left The School and that town and dropped the hate to look for this positive. I had to piece them together in some way. I had to piece them together into a rough draft, and then sentence by sentence put the whole thing together across the black ribbon. And then the piece would have to be read, and re-read and notes in the margin, and then read again and then at last finally typed and made out into the final draft, just as I wanted it. After that it would be out of my system, and all that remained of it would be a few notes in a notebook jotted down for possible use on some future, not yet known, occasion. If I wanted to know what I had said, or how I got this passage across I would, just like any other reader, have to take the book down from the shelves and search for the passage, and then read it. Maybe then I'd be able to remember how I had arrived at that method of communication, and perhaps even what the weather was like on the day I typed out the first draft. But once the notes had been put together and the unused put back and the undeveloped jotted down that, as far as I would be concerned emotionally, would be the end. It would be finished. That particular passage would be out of my system. Reading it through, even in my own final draft typing, would be as cold as reading a book by QWE or RTY. The fact that I had written it would have no effect on me whatsoever, except every now and then a painful wince, a tinge of embarrassment — did I really put that down, and in that way? — I find it very hard to read what I have written once it's in print. It's much harder even than reading it in final typescript and that I find by no means easy. By the time it reaches the presses I have moved on, way past the stage when six, twelve months ago on scraps of paper and in notebooks made up in a town I haven't ever been back to, the whole affair was living and vital and wonderfully important and immediate. Once in print it seems unalterable, unsmudgeable as if it has been stamped all over in every phrase with *Imprimatur — Nihil Obstat** and I

---

* Catholic doctrine, a declaration that a book is free of moral error.

feel like writing lies, lies, lies all over the front page because I don't feel quite like that any more, nor do I think along that line. There has been a movement and nothing will be quite the same again.

Back to this story of how a section came across the ribbon. I spread the pieces from the file over the carpet and all the tables and chairs. There was a fragment from a novel, from a short story, from notebooks, and I wandered on tip-toe across the room trying to work some order, some pattern into the fragments. I worked on ways of merging the pieces together. I almost reached the stage of desperation — when all the bits are typed and I go round the floor with a pair of scissors cutting out the words, phrases, sentences, passages that fit, that are relevant. I didn't quite get to that stage, but very nearly. Then with all the original and re-copied and rehashed pieces still spread out but in a much different pattern across the carpet and chairs I went out for something to eat. Then I came back and burnt all the rehash and recopy and no use for pieces and put the remainder in the folder and marked it 'straight cut Liverpool', which is just a fancy way of saying — type out as in the order given these pieces on Liverpool just as it stands only use your head as you type.

When I am tired, I often use these fancy ways. It helps to break the monotony, and relieve some of the frustration. I left it at that. Then some days later as I was moving through a preliminary draft in complete typescript I reached the point where the notes on Liverpool were intended to come in. I decided to type it as it said on the folder, straight, fragment on fragment just as they came in the folder. I won't put any dates to the pieces. Certain impressions and ideas will get repeated, but that is inevitable. I shall not even mark where one passage ends and the next begins. It would complicate the straight-cut pattern. The only changes that have been made have been in reading before typescript and are negligible.

.   .   .

Liverpool: Good Friday, 1958 — the city of ships, the port — that grisly reminder that from Liverpool one sails for darkest Africa, South America, and that land of the free on the other side of the ocean. Liverpool: sailors and dockers: grim, grisly, dirty, grimy, stealing, screaming, wide and winding like the Mersey from the oil plants down by the Cast Iron Shore, the promenade at Aigburth, the holes in the wall, the Dingle, the hole in the ground where the overhead railway has been ripped away, Pier Head, and the passenger docks down to Gladstone, and Pier Head. Pier Head — the green dirty buses to Litherland and Speke — the converging streets, Rodney, Nelson, Pitt, Grafton, Hope, Paradise, Pier Head; your last glimpse of England. Quick, quick, scurry away from the barren plaza to Tenerife, Brooklyn, Manaos, Buenos Aires, the trip up the Amazon, along the Guinea Coast, into the Hudson River. Robin had gone. It was there in the paper. It was there in black and white: L. Liverpool, F. New York, Mar 22. Gone. Robin had gone, the unalterable fact; and he was in Liverpool; he the swish, the chi chi, the snazzly, razzly young man, the secretary to that agency. Liverpool: here it was, the last outpost of England before one reached the swamps of Sierra Leone, Eire, the Amazon; before one saw the Statue of Liberty, the barren blank sameness of Manhattan, the Calle

Floride, Rio de Janeiro. Here it was: Pier Head, the Liver Building, the monument to business carried on in dingy rooms by gaslight by the emaciated clerks of a century ago. The Cunard Building, the monument to the public lavatory period. St. George's Hall — "Freemen have established a place for the Arts, Laws, and Councils." A business deal, a diplomatic handshake beside a Dorian pillar, beneath a Pre-Raphaelite monster. The Adelphi; Lewis' with that statue; Cresswell Mount rising above Scotland Road. The lions from St. George's glaring impotently down Lime Street, so very much more true to the decade than the white Victoria who beams down a red-tarmac Mall in London. The Braddocks, the building for the workers, each aerated box with its telly as big as your head.

And there in the paper beside 'Today's Business Done', the agony column, the Liverpool Stocks, Liverpool Cotton, the Mersey Shipping; the little blocks of news of the scouse, the whack, the English, the British, the universal: 'George Jonathan England, aged 51, of no fixed abode was further remanded in custody accused of assaulting Maggie May with intent to ravish her in Sefton Park on March 17th.' It was headed — 'Rape on St. Patrick's Day'. He thought of a subtitle — *Mortal Sin in Irish Capital, Englishman accused*.

He crossed the street, and dropped his paper into the gutter. The shop bell rang.

"Could I have a couple of hot cross buns please?"

"You wanna couple?"

The voice was fat, Irish. The street was Scotland Road, lean and above him stood the decomposed lettering on a derelict wall 'GOD IS LOVE'. On the pavement was the writing in pink, watery chalk — 'J.G. LOVES P.S. TRUE'. True, true, a fact, Robin had gone. True, the newsboard by the wall — 'ALL human nature, ALL of life is here — THE NEWS OF THE WORLD'.

Once, not so long ago, he had been part of all that — coming out at the age of fifteen from the care of the convent, orphaned into Camden Town, Cable Street, the chips wrapped up in the sad story of the Swindon school mistress and the young man from County Donegal. It was a different city, but the story was the same — the tatty bars on Williamson Square, the piano, the drums, the old lady singing, a wart on the end of her nose, hair on her chin. If you were the only girl in the world, and I was the only boy, I would dream, dream of a Garden of Eden where, where what wonderful, wonderful things we could do, just me and you — all the girls together now, one, two, three — Liverpool, London — they were part of the same jungle.

Outside the shop was a slot machine — ball-gum a penny — turn a flaking chromium handle on to one side and a picture in colour of Elvis down on the farm; and to the other Tommy Steele in black and white with the kids next door. For a penny.

A hot cross bun, freshly defrosted.

It was Good Friday — three hours on your knees. They had taught him that; a holy day of obligation, rotting women with coloured scarves tied over their cheap-perfumed hair, a rosary in their little bags, the *Pange Lingua*, the kissing of the cross, the relic, adoration, the hope, belief, paradise. They

---

* Catholic hymn, *Pange Lingua Gloriosi*.

could be street names. "GOD IS LOVE" crumbling on the wall across the street. On the paving stone by the ball-gum machine the rain was washing away the children's statement of love; true—the newsboard for ALL of life, the sodden picture of Elvis, faded. It lay there on the wet paving stone like a picture of the Sacred Heart that falls from the Missal, with the blessing of the favourite nun scrawled in red biro on the back—worship, belief—if only he could, had, if only there was a heaven. If only the sweetness on the land from Scotland Road to Cable Street, Williamson Square to Shaftesbury wasn't the pill with the bitter centre, the centre so bitter that it could blind any belief in a heaven of any kind, in a man capable of any reason, of any conscious kindness, or of love.

After eating the last hot cross bun he lit a cigarette and took the road south; a road of unbelief, without hope, without faith, the road of the too experienced, the road of those who are not conscious of what they are doing or saying, where religion and belief and hope are only street names; the road of the too broadly travelled; over the Mersey Wall—south to the Potteries, the Midlands, the garden city and public lavatory land and then home to his economic miracle, to London; all on his own to Chelsea Square. Robin had gone. Now he was alone, a position of trust at the end of the road, the long road with no arrival or departure points, only a series of dead and turning points, streets one believed in until one got there, and then—move on again.

Go north young man—Rugby, Stafford, Crewe—Liverpool. There's a copper passes you by. He turns round to you, and he says: "You look happy!" The cheek on it. Don't say owt. There might be a bye-law saying no cheek to officers of the law during the hours of darkness and before 9.17am I don't feel happy, but you get a sort of peace leaning on the railings and watching the convoys of buses pass you. I got echoes, memories ingrained in my marrow bones, all sweet and sour; associations of places with faces with an occasional thought or desire or wish. That half-cobbled street on Scotland Road, and there's Cable Street in London, a market square in the Midlands, squashed tomatoes. There's the tennies up and down and all over, and the slogans on the wall — Niggers Get Out — William Prince of Orange for Ever — We Need A Fast Boat to China to take the Yellow Peril Out — MacWonder feeds the millions to the god of war. There was a block in Gateshead, looking down on the Tyne; wandering through the washing on the top deck looking for this bird. There was a block in Birmingham — took me half an hour to get down, bleeding kids playing with the lift, the lift cage with me, just me in it. I tell you — who'd have kids. The endless grip of rubber on a leaf greasy road, the road north, south, east, west stretching like the twang of a guitar string. In the dawn, in the dusk, in the glow of orange lights. I can't cut out these vibrations, memories, superficial pictures, outward signs. The Mersey subway at James St. Station with its wooden platform. The Paris Metro. Cops in flat hats toting guns above the Chambre de Deputies before De Gaulle arrived. It's like as if jets of water were spurting at regular intervals on to the ear drum; drops of blood regularly pounding and bouncing off the retina like. Three days, four nights and no food. Only whisky, beer, cigarettes — the tongue, the teeth, the taste. It's like you drawn your guts up. These kids, in greasy black jeans and broken-back shoes screaming after me as I trail over Lime Street station forecourt — 'Spin a tanner skin' — little gels skipping after me and laughing and giggling and saying — "Put out the colours tonight". It makes you feel like a dirty old man, some rent collector who seduced your son and ran off with your daughter, and sent the daughter to bed for the geezers so he'd have the moola to hep with the son. Why did I come to this place in a blue fleck suit, of all the things to wear. What the hell?

That were the very first time I come to Liverpool. Must have been '57. I remember coming from Crosby by train. There was some meeting at a club. I'd got a message for a bloke. Got my trains all mixed up, that was why I was coming in from Crosby. Don't know how I got to Crosby. Got no idea. I can't remember much, but then I was in this train and there was blood all over, and a gash on my face, and there were blood in my mouth and there was an old lady sitting opposite, and the train rocked, and she kept saying dreadful, dreadful. I stood up, and says where are we, and she wouldn't tell me, but kept muttering away so I just hear her saying, dreadful, dreaful, all the time, dreadful, dreadful. I stood up and there was this blood all over, and all over my suit, and I looked in the mirror; it were just like my face had been used as a bit of cheese in a cheese scraper — there was skin and flesh and blood and grit and cuts and bruises and a great big black eye, a real shiner. I looked at this old lady, and I said I was sorry but I thought someone must have done me over, though I couldn't remember a thing like — and she just sat there with her little gloved hands all folded over her handbag muttering away—dreadful, dreadful—and I went out to the W.C. and I was sick. And when I got back we were coming through Widnes and Runcorn over the river like.

It's all an association, superficial, city to city, experience to experience, moving on from one affair to another, only retaining the quarter truth of one's own past, only being half-conscious, and not even knowing the broad direction of any possible personal future. It's the price of a hamburger in the round at Piccadilly tube station, and the drug stores open all night.

Look when you go in, she said, try and put on a Liverpool accent—it's different from Birkenhead you know, but don't say anything but ta and yeah if you can—and I'll say you're from over Walton like and she'll know then to keep her mouth shut. The old woman says do you wanna cup of tea, and I says yeah, and I had to drink this bloody great mug of tea that were all sweet. It looked like gravy and it tasted like a full bottle of saccharine, and it were a real pint-sized mug. And I had to drink it because if I didn't I'd have to say something.

Life needn't be like that. I could have caught the bus, and eat and sleep and the bus and the tube and the forms to fill in, and the lunch to get down you as fast as you can, and the dash to the sea and the flit back home, and the steady girl and all that, all that.

Stare, stare till you see nothing, neither the water not the oily darkness below, nor the sands, nor the sounds of the people. Stare until you see and hear and smell nothing. Stare until you feel nothing, and then jump and there, there will be nothing.

In the tunnel of love she screamed and held me tight, and I clutched at the roof and tore down a dragon's foot and she screamed again. A bell rang, and the doors clanged and the fair in its dodgem track glow was still there. I couldn't scream in that tunnel of love, it wasn't real. But the whirl of the fair outside it was darker and frightening and real dramatic, and more lovable and passionate than any tunnel of love. It all goes round and round like the whip, and she clinged to my body and I could feel nothing, nothing at all. She said, ooh, you aint half romantic; and I says you stupid cow; and she says ooh don't be like that; and so I says I'm not going to be, don't you worry your fat little head over that.

She came with me to the station. I said tataa, and she says come back; and I says I will and I gets in the train, and then she jumps up at me and gives me a great big peck on my cheek of all things, and so I slaps her down and she just looks and the train goes off darling, I don't feel a thing. I'll be back, yes, I'll be back but when I come back I won't want you. I'll be different. The place'll have changed. I'll have changed. And even if it aint; I won't ever want you again, you move on love, got to, so why get all romantic.

Flush the romance and drama away. I know I'm alive, biologically. I had my doubts once, but I'm sure enough of that now. And the rest, it doesn't matter. It doesn't concern me. I'm not bothered.

Woman and bras — the nipple of the bra showing — not the real nipple.

She puts her arm round me and she says, this black velvet she says — Darling, find out if I'm a woman or not. So I says; Darling, I don't like your kind of smell. I forgot, I was in Liverpool. It's William of Orange, not Sir Oswald.

Women in high-heeled shoes whose cheeks chop on their every tiny step. The calves of their legs touch. The nance walk of the office boys. The fancy walk of the others. The self-conscious, self-dramatization of the young men. The old man who smiles a good morning. The one you met the night before, and now you see in the light of the morning. The said truth hits home. It's ordinary.

The girl who holds her boy friend's hand. You would never have thought it if you knew him at school, and now she's in the family way, by him — there's no doubt about it — it was him. The men with stern faces in a great hurry. The copper. The negro Yank, chew spit chew, dark glasses. People in cars looking up at the clock above the tobacco store. The road sweeper, clean shaven, highly efficient, scornful and the pretentious hand signals.

The clock in the gas lamp ticking. That little something about landlords, the English ones of milieu caffs and pubs; like the Chinese, half apologetic, fully understanding, great wisdom, mouths closed.

The chip papers, the butt ends, the unwashed puke. In the darkness the riding lights of the ships on the river like yellow sparklers. The last buses in convoys; red Ribble, green Crosville; green Express Limited Stop City; No. 1 goes to Dingle. Police with hats like Caesar and Rome. Park Road and a caff — photos of Frankie Vaughan and Billy Fury, signed. James Street subway station. Vernons. The groups on the corner. Everton Valley. The merging of night and morning.

And I gets oom and she says to me — do you wanna use me — use you I says — no food no sleep, only p. and the odd reefer and whisky and beer and cigarettes and the juke box and love — and all to keep the act alive.

．　．　．

Go down a coalmine, go down the pit. It's like travel by air, one of those things. Without it you miss so much. Once you go down you can never forget it. It wasn't the face, or the cage that drops all that way from the top to the bottom, but the passages, the maze of twisting, twilight lanes, like the tunnel of love in real, this maze that meets you the moment you get out of the cage at the bottom and leave the main pit road behind. You walk, you crawl, you stumble with your head bent and your back aching, and the only light a yellow glow from your helmet to guide you, and then there would be a group of lights in front, and dust and doors and a rise in the height of the ceiling, and you'd stand up and stretch and relax and raise your head and see these figures, half-naked figures in white dusty boots. They'd stop work, to look at you as you passed. The old ones, they'd say their how do. You'd say your reply the same way. And then look at the young, the ones your own age, and they'd nod, and you'd nod back and that would be all. Say nothing. Nothing said. Nothing to say, and you'd move on through more doors, and bend your head down again, and you'd be alone, and it was pitch black bar the lamp like a headlight from your helmet.

That's how I felt on the top, on the surface; wandering across, on my own with only a shadow to talk to, and then I see a red glow in the sky, and I lift up my head and stretch and relax as I come to the town. And I say, how do, and cup of tea, and how much, and whisky—and the interesting faces, the new sights, the young, they just stare. I stare back. I say nothing. Nothing said. Nothing to say. There isn't time. There isn't any point. I'm just a visitor, passing through, moving on. I know my place, I know where I belong. Yet I want to stop, and sit down and wait for the silence to break and the first penetrating question to come out through the silence; to establish contact—who are you? Why have you come here? And at times all I can do is stare, stretch; all taut and tied up just stare; and then move on. I mustn't stay. I mustn't become involved. But I don't move. I stand still and stare. I want to start the ball rolling, ask my own first question—have a fag—but there isn't the chance. I've picked the wrong compartment. I'm in a non-smoker. I've got the wrong brand image on my fag packet. I must make an effort. Go out, buy the right fag packet. Find the right compartments. Must find the smokers. I have made my concessions. Now stand up and say your piece I am a stranger. I was only going to stay till they filled the car with petrol, but something of your place has caught me; I've been bitten. And now you see, I'm interested in this place. Please, will you show me around, take me to the interesting face, show me the vital place, give me a message, paint a picture, something that may add up, something I can take back, along, across with me.

No, I don't say this. It wouldn't be fair. I don't want to intrude. I know my place, and in any case I may have the right brand image now, but I still haven't found the formula for the opening words. I'm an anonymous guest, an uninvited visitor. There are no points of contact. I have sufficient respect to just sit. I won't butt in, offend, break up whatever private world there might be beyond your stare. And I'm a little frightened. I'm not at all sure what might happen if we got together. There might be an explosion that wouldn't be any good for either of us.

I am a visitor. I wrote in and said I wanted to go down the pit. You're stuck down there, and I'm not so you stare at me. I know you can see it, that I've fought through and come out alright, don't have to spend eight hours a day down the pit, I fought through and I got the nerve to flaunt this in your face. No, it's not like that. I have too much respect to want ever to forget the past, so I come down here; to see for myself, to keep in contact, to renew my belief. I know you can tell. So can I. It's like blue blood. No matter how you try to cover it up, you can always tell. And just because you're still down there you wish me bad luck. There are to be no how do's, just the stare and the silence, and the stubborn refusal to make contact, on both sides.

It's so much easier for the man who had no struggle, who never knew in any form what it was like down there, with the knowledge that down there was not an experience but a life, that there could be no getting out, or moving away without a very real miracle. It's alright for him. There are no inhibitions, no jealousies, no rivalry. There can be an acceptance. You know where he stands, apart, belonging to a higher caste.

But you see, I don't feel I do. That's the tragedy. I'm like a refugee. So we don't quite know where we stand. This is something rather new, we're not sure, not any of us. So the barriers go up, and the silence and the stares come down, for me. And contact, communication is an effort. But in spite of the effort, and possibly because of the effort I'm going to stay. I must stay until there has been a give and a take, a communication. Until I've been able to say — I know, I know. We know, we know; but alright, I'm the lucky one. I have the time and the ability and the energy to do battle, and that's what I'm doing. Don't throw me out.

And so I come up, and check into a hotel, and I hang around; and I use all the closed shop places of contact, but I say nothing. This is their pitch. They must make the breakthrough. Not me, they must make the opening crack, break the silence, start the talk. They must break down the barrier. I can't. Officially I'm the one who's moved up and out. It must be their privilege to open up, and their right to refuse. I haven't the audacity, or the nerve, or the right to do anymore than just walk in and sit down. And so I hang around, waiting, and then all of a sudden walking down a sidestreet, standing at a bar, the walls come down, and they make the first moves: Where you come from? Nowhere. Where you going? Nowhere. You gonna stay here? Maybe. What for? I haven't a home. This is as good as anything. What you do for a living? The past, memories, investments.

I'm not made welcome. I'm not taken in. I'm accepted at my own face value — the daft bloke staying at the hotel. I've given nothing away. I've said nothing. But I've laid an atmosphere of mystery, drama — aroused curiosity. Checkmate. You move next.

Maybe, this all seems cruel and unnecessary. No, I don't think so, and in any case it's a bit of an exaggeration. You see, it's aroused interest, and put the work of contact out of my hands. Look, they aint going to make me into an uncle, or a white collar worker, or a journalist, or anything. I'm me, and me with a vengeance. I shall make the effort only if I'm forced. I'm quite willing to be forced. Then and only then, if you ask me will I put the cards on the table. I prefer to have to go through all these stares and silences, because it works off my own embarrassments. It helps me. I couldn't do this open, cool, detached, sociological question and answer stuff. And in any case I'm not really interested in the answers, I don't want just information. I want the tone, the attitude; and for the interest to be worked up till I'm in the dock and they're doing all the asking. It must be two way. I haven't come to mine and take away for my personal use and gain. If there's going to be any use or gain it has to be two way, and from me the individual to you the individual.

You see, out of necessity we must get together; we have to mix but it must be as two individuals, person to person. By all means, set me apart, after all I'm in a class on me own; but don't don't put me in a little box, as one of a caste, as one of a kind because I am not. I'm like you. I'm on my own. I'm in a class all of my own. A class that consists of one person, just me.

nine

I FIND THE MUSIC, FIND THE WORDS. I PUT THEM together and get them just as I want them. But it takes a long while, and a lot of moving about. All this moving about, it's like waiting for some outer direction to set the words to the music, music that spells cash and freedom and all that.

It's like being a pop star. You stand up there on the stage. You move your finger, to the right — a simple action — and you're terribly conscious of it; conscious of a sort of inner audience that is watching, not critically but just watching like an echo that will come back to make yourself into the critic. You're alone in a great white spot, and hearing the band start up, and the backing group going aah, aah, and you take the mike into your hands. I have got to sing, and you think of the words, and then you look out towards where the people are and you swing in, and make noise, and go just wild and you see people watching you, some of them just staring, taking it all in, and some of them being very clinical; only you can't see them for the white light blinds you. You can only feel them, and they're watching, watching hard because they don't know your next move, and they think that you ought to; that even if they don't know which way you're going to move next, then you will. I mean, everybody thinks that you know what you're doing, only they're so wrong. But then I tell you what I'm going to do next and you don't believe me. You keep on looking. I keep thinking, now you want a surprise, and the band starts up and I keep trying to think. I must get the words straight, compose, work out what I want to say — but you keep looking. I know you're looking, and I don't want to disappoint, or fail to surprise or hold you, so I go on bash, bash, all wild — take this while you're waiting, take this and like it.

There's something so very wonderful and vital about a singer, be it Yves Montand, Cliff Richard, Judy Garland, Sinatra, Elvis, Ella. The pop concert, so different from a straight music concert like a symphony or a jazz; the whole thing gets personalised. The message that comes across and through is that of the star of the show, not an idea or a theme, or a general feeling, or a collection of sounds. A link has to be forged between the star and the individuals of the audience. If the link isn't made; if the thing doesn't get across then the results are immediate. It's not a rejection slip from an agent, or a no-sale ticket from a publisher but a knife thrown at the stage to hit not an idea, or a sound but a person. The reaction and the response are made clear there and then, at once. There is an immediacy there isn't with the TV, or the film or a book.

Maybe 2,000 people go to the Hall for the one-night stand of the star show. Assume fifty per cent of these have come to look, to clinically analyse, to take the mick; that is, there are in the audience 1,000 sociologists at work, cranks, statisticians, amateur and professional talent scouts, et cetera et cetera. That still leaves 1,000 people who have come to take in person the message, the rhythm, the beat of the star whose image they have cottoned on to; the legend they've picked up in the TV magazine, movie; the gossip wise. They know some part of the legend. They have an image of you, what you will do, what you will be like.

> *Paul Robeson — Old Man River — Keep the Red*
> *Flag Flying — big black man.*
> *Judy Garland — A Star is Born — Somewhere Over*
> *the Rainbow — tragedy, female.*
> *Creature X — male — teen — lean.*

So, there are about 1,000 people who have come for the message, to get uplifted, to be reconverted, to take a night off, to see the live show. There are 1,000 people who are going, up to a point, to take in wholesale the show and the star of the show, or just the star.

I'm not interested now with the funny ha ha show, or the satirical shows, or the Tommy Steele, Tom Lehrer; or even the plain variety shows like the Perry Como thing which are better on TV and let's hope they stay for ever as unlive as that.

I am concerned with the great religious shows, the romantic, the heroic, the ones where you can forget; immerse yourself with another person; the union with you shows.

Ella, Edith, Nat, Cliff, I have come to cry with you because you get across to me just how I feel when I'm not able quite to put into words or actions how I feel; when I can find no form to put what I feel into. You see I'm ordinary brown card 797 in the crowd. I am married to XY. I am married because I didn't want to feel and to be alone, and reading those poems about the pee stains on the underwear frightened me; and also let's face it, please, getting married is the most respectable and the most permanent way known to man of getting his oats. I am ordinary working chap X leading the life any man in the street, any brown card on the shop floor would lead. Ella, show me show me what life could have been, up and down, happy and sad; a life with a spontaneity and a movement and a generosity, and a living pitch and depth of feeling, show me this. Show me life through coloured spectacles, because that is how I wanted it, how I still want it, and how I only find it one day, even if that, in the 365. Take me away from my daylight and fluorescent white light life, and show me the spectrum; take my functional spectacles away from me. Just for tonight let me dare to leave my functions and my self-inflicted tasks at home. Do not let me for one moment see life as it is for me; but throw in the drama, the punch, the goodness, the fun, the glory, the greatness, the bad, the moment of passion, the moment of despair. Tell me all about them deep blues, and tell me like Judy Garland that somewhere over … Yes, I wanted to go there. When I was a child I wanted to go there. I saw *Peter Pan* at Christmas time in a provincial theatre that is now a supermarket, and I wanted to be like Peter Pan; to never grow up; never have to see straight; never have my blinkers put on. I want to go there, be like Peter Pan. Even now I want this. But I couldn't. I was afraid, and now I can't. It's too late. I'm young only in heart. I am just X in the crowd at seat NO. J17 Circle of the show on tour calling at this place for one night, two shows, and then on.

I cannot book the whole front row for the Floyd Patterson fight. I could not even fill the front row with my supporters, or even loyal friends, or even enemies. I don't know anybody.

I am no Sinatra. I sit at Hall K, Town Z, seat NO. J17 Circle, and I wish and dream. I want to go to that beautiful land where the lemonade springs from the soda water fountain, and the cigarette trees ... Let me fly round the earth like the first cosmonaut, and leave this world to the sounds of this world, and then with the greatest of ease in a red velvet chair recline to the heavenly music of love, relayed from Cairo or Moscow or Rome, it wouldn't matter. It would seem as if it came from the heavens themselves, and being out in a cosmos like Peter Pan: one moment of ecstasy, of timelessness, of weightlessness, love infinity. But then, you get up there, go round one, two, three, and then down, and they change the music, and come down to the Northern Lights of Old Aberdeen; Motherland, Motherland I Can Hear You Calling; Keep the Red Flag. You know if I was up there all timeless and weightless and enjoying it all and they started playing the Yellow Rose of Texas, or God Bless the Prince of Wales or something like that, I'd want a button to press to burn me and the whole thing up. You couldn't come down to that.

It's strange, that for all the efforts of the Elders of our tribes to provide the younger generation with fitting and suitable heroes, we've got heroes in a set of unzipping the banana young men, and women of maturity to cuddle and comfort the poor banana once it's bin unzipped, and young girls who look like boys. But let's be honest, all the Soviet achievements, they're a little unsatisfying, emotionally. The moralists have tried to provide the world with honest, happily married two kids, secondary modern to tec at night and skilled technocrat to Party member and Government commission sitter; provincial ordinary suburban ever so nice and normal, fit and healthy and the heroes are still a long list of Ishmaels. The figure is on the stage, the banana, the Boy-god, the Ishmael. The backing starts up. He moves into a solitary blue spot. He cannot sing, talk, express; but the youth and the beauty he has are worth more than all the other qualities he does not have. The other cerebral and emotional qualities we can have all through life, but the youth and the beauty are over before you have the chance to put them across. He moves alone across the desert of the stage. It is the face, the look, the loneliness, the uncommunicable, unclubable — the figure we would all like to be or be in physical contact with — tall, dark, slim. Letting in a little light, bringing in a little life. With our 7/6's we must buy him and kill him and then love the image and read the magazines and start all over again.

For every sale there is a price, and this price is the desert. He stands like Billy Budd and we cry out as he sits on his stool to say 'I wanna be loved by you, by you'. Yes, me, me, we are gone. We are round the bent bend. He won't come down. He can't. He must wait for us, for us the judge and the jury and the god to crucify him, and his only hope can be through a resurrection in the magazines; an eternal and indivisible and twice nightly sacrifice. He looks all lonesome and blue and we cry out to him to come down from the cross. There's a flicker of a smile across his face. After all, he's paid to be crucified twice nightly, and the mood changes and he annoys us. Like Dorian Gray he is conscious of his looks and his body and soul (the mind and the emotions are not important); of his every-thing and our feelings, our emotion. It is we who are all alone, and we are not paid professional martyrs. We do not have the riches, the little compensations his public loneliness has brought him. Save us, save us—and others and our own other halves, say come down from your perch. You say you send them, send yourself. Oh Boy call the tune for us and make us happy, and we shall give ourselves to you. We fall prostrate on the edge of the stage, and he smiles and throws us a flower some disciple threw him some hours ago, and then the spotlight dies and the curtain comes down, and the band plays *God Save the Queen* and we are helped to stand straight by the impartial police, and that is the end of the show.

The lonely boy is physical. It is we and not the artist who have to supply the emotion, the thoughts, the feelings. All he does is give us the body and the soul, the centre of an idea. As we grow older we can't hope for anything that perfect. We can't hope anything like that will come our way, and in any case even if it did we wouldn't have the price we would need to pay. We know that there are no oases in the desert, no desert islands in the sea; only oil wells that spurt out a black liquid and twist tall Texans and cover the earth with a blackness and a part of it with money, to become a part of the jungle man prepares to give back to his god. There is no heaven on earth, no dream to come true. But still we turn to the lonely boy; in the city but not of the city. We can only hope that out of our dull ordinary lives there may come not only the one-night stand, and the movie and the magazine and the art, but the real, one little compensation to make up for the rest, one knife thrust deep enough to hurt, one tense moment to remember. Your wife is dead. You mourn. You cry. But there are the bills to pay, the solicitors to see, and funeral directors and the arrangements to attend to, the notice to put in the paper, and there is no sick pay.

Love—you wait for the turn of the key in the door, that never comes. You wait for the steps in the hall, for the bell to ring. You have gotten the blues and you wanna cry. There is the train to catch, the office—no time to mourn. I cried a river over you. I waited ten, eleven, twelve o'clock scanning every train, bus, car, taxi, and motor-cycle, waiting for you but you didn't turn up. There was no message and no arrival.

You don't really wait that long. You're very upset. You're moody, annoyed; but you take the coach back all the miles you came, mourning the unnecessary expense, and the things like weeding those rows of peas, or reading that novel that you might have done if you had known in advance that the journey would be fruitless. You turn up at the office after a restless night dreaming of the things you might have done if there had been an arrival. You go back home and ask: any post, any post, anyone call, anyone call, any message, a telegram? But life goes on. We are the crowd. We are brand X. The nearest we can get is the banana. We give up the waiting and the no arrivals. We give up the great hopes of a real, and marry and settle down and moan. One night we went to bed, and I did not take the usual precautions and we made such love and all the time I was dreaming of a banana and there was a child. This child will never know that he had three parents—me and you and the banana, and perhaps your banana too. It has three, and maybe it has four. If only we knew who the banana was. Illegitimate births have nothing, nothing on banana babies—there's the tragedy, not in the bastard.

We have come here tonight, Ella, Nat, Edith, Judy, Frankie, Boy, for you to tell us how we felt or could have felt when she didn't turn up. We who have often wanted, but never dared to sit up all night over the whisky bottle. We who have not physically cried over a broken heart, have come to hear you put the words to the music, the expression to the feeling, the lines of definition to our vague sensations, to our half-sensed and unexplored desires. We did not cry through the wee small hours. We went to bed and slept; but we would have cried if we hadn't duties, responsibilities, and the 7:55. The factory, the office, they dictate every day of our lives, bar Saturday nights, Sunday mornings and the Bank and Big Holidays.

.   .   .

Now you turn the tempo, and tell us she's gone. So what. I'll walk down the street and find myself another gel. We have wanted to do that too, but when we've finished work we haven't the energy for owt but a tart who is paid to do all the work. And in any case, look: I don't have that kind of money; the cash you need to be sure that what you pick up hasn't got, well to be sure there's no contamination, like. Why worry? I may have lost my religion, but not my sense of common decency, or common British standards of cleanliness. I still wash my hands. Why worry? I do, and that's enough. I've been trained to worry.

And so we go out of the show, and get into our cars, and we wind the window down, lose our tempers — why don't you look where you're going, lunatic — you looking for an early grave my man — there ought to be better car parks — where's the police — Darling, he was wonderful. He was wonderful. I enjoyed that show. Give me a kiss? Not while you're driving, Henery, please. You still love me? Of course I love you.

Got to see our man at Bromsgrove tomorrow. I hate going to Bromsgrove. I still love you, darling. Good night. Out.

He stands in the wings, butterflies in his guts like he was a Christian being thrown to the lions, and they're going to eat you, not the act or the methods or the coming across, but you. You want to go out there with a little placard, like in a Medieval Cycle saying 'Eating People is Wrong' and just walk right across the stage, and then go back to see that the groups are ready to start up with The Queen. But the band starts up and the theme music comes out, the cue, and on you go, because you have been trained to go on, and you get paid to go on, and what would the papers say, and you have a duty to the hungry fans.

You are on, and there is the sense of being a Christian in the lions' arena; of being a pawn in someone else's hands — the lions are there, but you are protected and you know you are a fake Christian, a fake matador, put on to give the impression because the supply of real or even neo-Christians has run out. I say I belong to you, the Crowd, but it isn't true. I belong to Daddy, my Dear Sugar Daddy, that Man you never see, that man with the fat cigar.

You may belong to that man, but it is you who have this sense of power. You have the glory and the fame and the honour — you move your leg and they scream — that wonderful sense of power, of knowing that they love you and as long as the nylon thread that keeps the vital seams in your pants holds tight they will love you no matter what you do or say, or sing; as long as they don't hear too well, see too close;

as long as they can have that feeling that what you are saying, is what they want you to say, what they themselves feel but wouldn't dare to say.

You have only one thing to sell—and that is your young body, but that is sufficient. That is what they want, and that is what they must think they are getting. The show in the flesh. They must think they could have touched you. They have come to see you in the flesh, and they must take back the idea that they have. They must see that you can speak and sing and walk and that your muscles work and that you are alive all the way through, and that there is nothing but the flesh. And it is you, and not the man with the cigar that gets the sense of power when you know what your flesh can do to people out there; the sense of power in being a banana, the sense of power in a physical body that can make up for a poverty and lack of imagination in the act, the beat, the theme; the sense of power in seeing and knowing that with your flesh alone you can get across.

And all those people, all that fifty per cent believe that you love them, and they take it all in and they are so wrong. Because you are cool and calculating and operate like a high-powered organization. You exist to make money, and you have worked out a rhythm, a discipline that gives you the freedom they don't have, and the money they don't have, and the sense of achievement and of having done something that they don't have. They are so wrong.

And all that other fifty per cent who think that you don't love the crowd at all, they too are wrong, so very wrong. They talk of the camp and the Cadillacs, and the man with the big cigar, and the hypocrisy. They don't know that you believe in what you are doing, that you get a sense of achievement in getting across entertainment, in getting the flesh across — and they are going back to their offices to talk and be camp and deride and they don't know. You love it and you believe in it, and you worship it and if the man with the big cigar is there, it is because you wanted him to be there. If you have bin corrupted, then it was with your own consent and it wasn't corruption. But they don't know this.

And tomorrow you go off to work yourself, to another town, to another record or magazine session, another talk with the men with the cigars and the PR boys and the technicians and specialists who keep you going, and who you keep going. Tonight you rest and read the magazines because it interests you to find out what your latest move or affair is, when you live in a world where you don't have time for affairs. But they don't know that. They never will. That's the way it is. Only a few will break through and join in the secret and they will keep it carefully guarded, though in fact it wouldn't greatly matter if they let the whole shoot out because no one would understand, and even if they understood they wouldn't believe, and even if they believed it wouldn't make much difference. Boy, it's a wonderful life. It's great to be young.

We worship the banana and we think it real. That's where we fall down. We worship the banana and the banana worships other bananas. This is all true, but for The Banana there are little compensations. For him there's a job he likes doing; enough money to live on plus a certain freedom, a certain and wonderful sense of freedom, sense of achievement, of fulfilment; the chance to work out for oneself a rhythm of life, not a rhythm dictated by a never-ending, never-changing production line. It is better to be The Banana than to be a reader of the unzip bit on the wall.

And me? Yes, I too want to stand up there. Stand up there and get rid of, pour out. Stand up there and give out all, everything that I have found on my skins, everything I have seen in the mirror and wished to remember. I want to stand up there and give out the fast bits, and the slow; the hot and the cool. Just simply because it makes me feel good when I have poured it all out. It's like going to see a psychiatrist, only instead of me paying out, I'm the one who stands to get paid.

I want to stand up there all arrogant and assured and tell the blur beyond the lights, the blur in the cigarette fug, I do not want to be like you. I don't want to be ground down. Don't drag me down. And when the bastards get their hands on you, you've got to fight them, and fight them or you'll get dragged down until you just don't matter not even to yourself. I want to stand up there and rock and gyrate, not at or to an audience but in the presence of an audience; and not for an audience but for myself. I want to stand up there and tub thump, and work out and explore myself and what I see around me. It won't be for the audience. It's just that with a blurred fug beyond the lights, with the presence of an audience I feel best and I work best.

But all art is prostitution. And putting into form, or coherence, or finding a pattern for a life that is incoherent and a world that has no pattern is a sort of prostitution. I'm not selling what I believe, or my country, or my class, or what I see but the way I see things, the how I believe; the meanderings and wanderings before I reach the stage where I can sit in front of the black ribbon in solitude.

And yet I'm afraid to stand up there in the blue spot. I feel lonely and unworthy, and not quite right. I feel I should be able to face the blur out there like a strip dancer or a politician, with facts and statistics and statements, something tangible, something worth the money you've paid at the door. Look, let me come down we'll all sit together and watch another show. Look, I'll phone up this tart I know. Look, I'll send a car round to this MP I know, and they'll come and do a turn and we'll all get value for money. Look, they're experts. I'm only an amateur. Look, I'm coming down into that auditorium. I'm not going on with the advertised programme. I don't want to meander and wander and shed skins in front of you, and ask myself all these questions. It isn't fair to do this to me, and you'll not get your money's worth. Look, this tart she'll satisfy you, this MP. I know he'll charm you and show you the statistics, and he'll give you something.

Sir, we paid to see you, not some friend of yours. We want to see you, your wanderings, the you beneath the skin; the you in search of what those friends of yours think they have found, but we feel they haven't. We don't want to be satisfied tonight. We want to find out how you get your satisfactions. We have paid our money to see you dance, and that is what we want to see. We have come out of genuine curiosity to see how and what you perform. You see we don't know your statistics. We want to see if you have any.

And so I stand up there, and I start to sing and I hear my voice going out to the absorbent fug, to the faceless auditorium; and all the while a voice is coming back at me and it isn't an echo. It's questions coming back at me about what I've just sung about; questions I'd ask if I was in the auditorium at this same time as I am on the stage.

It's like I was a politician, coming down the steps from a flight from somewhere, some conference or meeting and all around after the flash bulbs burst were those faceless men, these blurred figures and they were saying things; and I knew I had to say my piece, but I couldn't get it out right, and every time I got half way through I started asking myself questions, whether what I was saying was true, what relevance, what effect. And then I lost for ever what I should have said and started talking to myself, out loud about how difficult it was getting used to the time back here, and how the thing I was supposed to say was written before I left and I needn't have gone, because I didn't see anything really. But I had this dream on the way back. I wanted to see this old girl friend of mine. I thought about her when I was over there, and I should like to see her again. You're conscious of all the men around you, and their questions but it doesn't penetrate. You're conscious of You being in the middle of them, and not of them as individuals or people; only that they are blocking out my picture of You. Their questions get in the way. You want them to take a seat, and listen and shut up. I want to start talking to myself, and then something will come out in the end. Their questions keep coming at you, but they don't penetrate. Only your own questions come back. It's like when you've waited three hours for her, and you've at last given up, and you go past the taxi rank and someone says that you've been waiting a long time and she won't come now. The questioner has the best intentions, and is very kind but the question doesn't go in. You want to take him by the hand and say, I had that feeling she wouldn't turn up, because you see last time I saw her, last time we met she ... and tell him all the tale, but there isn't time; and half way through even if you could start he wouldn't have heard your tale going in, but things that happened to him like this that is happening to you will all get mixed up with your tale, and by the end the only thing you will have achieved will be to have dragged up his own past. He won't know anymore about you, except that you are in some ways, in the basic like him. But he'll know a bit more about himself. I suppose that even if that took place it would have been worth the effort in telling the story.

That last sentence is rot.

You take him by the arm not because you want him to listen, but because you want to tell him, full stop. If I stand up on this stage and tub thump and churn, and you go away with nothing, but at the end I feel relieved, like I've coughed up all the bad beer then it's alright. It has been worth it. I have closed the lav door, and I have taken paper, and when I have finished with the paper and washed my hands I shall feel lighter and freer. But I hope, I think this is where I fail, you can read the paper. Remember only the duplicate sheets you will never see are really like toilet paper. The top sheets is, oh yes, quite definitely art. That's the pity. And so I stand with this blur beyond the lights affecting me. I stand and ask myself questions, again and again.

ten

ASK MESELF QUESTIONS — YOU'RE JOKING, OF COURSE
— I tell you, I tell you, after that thing bust up, that thing in
Leicester, I wandered all over the place, and in the end when
I couldn't face borrowing off other people no more I quit
my floating, and I come back this town, and I knew I'd be
unhappy as hell in this place. You know why? I tell you.
There's two things I hate — poverty and pain, but the worst of
them's being poor. I was in a mess, a real mess so I went back
where I knew I could live cheaper than I could anywhere else,
and I started out on the first day I got back looking for a job.

I went down the Labour Exchange. Have you got any jobs
— what you been doing — so I told them the truth — so they
says, no nothing like that. So, I says look man I says look I'm
after a job, any job. I'm broke and worse. My bloody pride's
gone, even if I ever had any. I'm bust. I've got to have a job.
So he looks at me and he says, don't you talk like that. You
want a proper job, what with your education and all that. I
could have hit him. I could have hit him right over the other
side of the town to Bradlaugh's statue. Because of your education. He could see I didn't like this, so he said if anything
came along he'd let me know. I leaves him my name and
address and well, he couldn't have been fairer than that, or
could he?

Well, after this had happened about ten, twenty times. I counted up to fourteen. I never bothered to count any more after that. Every morning for two solid weeks, bar Saturdays and Sundays, I trudged the streets. Every bloody night, four o'clock, I'd go through the paper looking for owt. But then I was daft. There were things and places I daredn't try, like the Brewery where the students worked. All the jibes, all the cat calls; I probably wouldn't have got any, but just having to tell the Leicester story once more, it would have killed me. Goes up to this shoe place. They wanted an invoicing clerk. Nine to five, plenty of free time, just the job, nice, right. So I goes up the reception and there's this woman and I gives her my name, and she says—Ooh she says, you're the young man who had the black eye. Read all about you in the papers. Did it hurt very much, that black eye? No darling. I never stayed for that job. I was down them stairs before I lost my temper.

Well, this went on for fourteen days. The railway company wouldn't have me, even them. After that I started out again, on the Monday in my third week of job hunting. I was walking up this street and I see this leather-dressing firm and I remembered as in the paper they wanted machine operators or something. So I finds the office, and this mask face of a girl comes out and says—yees—I says I wonder if there's any chance of a job. So she says—I'll have to see. There's a little wait and then this man comes out and we go out in the yard.

Worked in leather before?

No. Where you worked before?

Working in this rubber place over Leicester. Left it. Wanted to come back home (you have to use your imagination).

What were you doing in rubber?

(Bastard). Er, a bit of everything like, working on machines.

What sort of machines?

(Rubber, rubber-yeah.) Moulding machines.

What sort of factory? (Jesus, he went on and on; and that was the first time I'd gone right out and told a straight lie.)

Then he says:

How much were you earning?

About twelve, thirteen and then with overtime about fifteen sometimes.

Well, we can't offer you anything like that.

I thought — look, mate, brother, comrade, just offer me a job, a fiver a week and I'll take it. I'm rock bottom. I need a job.

Then he thinks.

Er, yes, well we can offer you about eight, nine to start with, and then we'll see how you get on.

I says when can I start.

Wednesday if you can.

No, look I can start Thursday. Only you see Wednesday I've fixed up to go up London. I mean, I'd got a free meal waiting for me in London and I'd got a bit of business to do, so I told him that if he didn't mind I'd start on the Thursday. He said that he didn't mind, so it was all fixed. But never once he'd asked me if I'd got any cards, or tax form or anything like that.

He wasn't too bad. He was a Tory councillor, and they ran an all-white factory. Never admit it, but they'd never set a coloured fellow on. And there wasn't any really well-organised union. Family business it was. But when I leave that place I'll have to leave alright with him because although he'll never know it he saved me with that job. I was really down.

Well, I gets there for my first morning and I looks round at the other blokes. Not a single person I knew. I'd stick to the rubber tale, and I keep my North Midland accent. I bin there five months so far. I got two more to do, and so far no one has said owt about the past.

But I think some of them know now. There's this foreman. He says to me one day. You went to the grammar school didn't you? I said bold as I could, no I never. I never went school here. He looks at me all old-fashioned. But he never said owt like that again.

And then there were two of the gels. They started on at me one day, but they never carried on. And after that they never asked me no questions like that any more.

I wanted it that way. I just didn't want to explain to another person any more. If I was going to put it all down it was going to be on paper, no other way. I'll be so bloody glad when the time comes when I can move off again. So glad. When I can come down to being me again. It gets so lonely here. I told them the story to protect myself, and I've stuck to it, and I'm going to keep it up right through to the time when I leave the whole town. I'm like a stranger in this town. I've never felt so much of a stranger as I do in this town. I've never felt so much of a stranger as I do in this place, and working where I do; and yet I was born here. I'll be so glad when I leave.

I get up about half past six without any alarm and I go downstairs and make a pot of tea, and I cut my pack up. I never take more than three sandwiches. There isn't time to eat any more than three. I take an apple if there's one to spare. If I can't I'll beg one off this lad I know who's on the market. I have my cornflakes, and they are nice, but the milk, it's usually a day old, a bit off. But you don't have to grumble too much. I like cornflakes, now and then. I light a cigarette, the cheaper brand, though I never have to buy them in packets of five, well not usually at any road. I don't mind them. They're not a bad smoke. But I don't particularly like cheap cigarettes, it's just that they cost less. I go out and walk down the street with my pack up in my pocket, and sometimes a bit of sugar or tea if I forgot to buy any dinner times. I feel just like a mole when I come out at about seven. I never have a proper wash in the mornings. I never clean my teeth in the mornings. There isn't really time. I have a swill, and throw water over my hair to get the sleep out. But there's oftener than not still sleep in my eyes when I come out so I try to rub it out on the way to the bus stop. My mouth's still a bit cloggy with tea, and scraps of flakes and the taste of milk, all on top of that just woke up taste. The cigarette usually puts that right. There isn't time really to finish the second cup of tea, so almost always I leave half of the second behind. Never got round to only pouring out a half cup. I just pour out a full one and then I have to leave half, because I must catch the five-past seven bus at the top of the street. I get on the bus, and up into the top deck with my cigarette alight.

The one thing that hits you, even if all the windows on the bus are open and it's the hundredth or thousandth trip on the

early morning bus, is the smell of hair cream and hair oil. It's
dreadful. The moment you go up on to the top deck it hits
you. I think it's the most lousy smell I know. You come out,
your mouth all clogged and your nose all clogged, and stiff all
over your back and legs, and you've lit a fag to try and get rid
on it, and then this sweet, sticky smell hits you — hair cream.
It's vulgar. I say how do to a couple of people I know more or
less vaguely, faces that haven't got a name but you see them on
that bus every day. I do my best to keep myself to myself. Try
only to speak when I'm spoken to, and then if I can find a way
round it I'll say nothing. I glance quickly at the others, pale,
tired faces of the a.m. bus. Sometimes a pipe-smoker gets on.
That's bad. Pipe smoke upsets you, don't go well with the
milk and the cornflakes. People who clean their teeth before
they go to work have told me that it don't go very well with
toothpaste either, this aroma of pipe tobacco. Always comes in
great big puffs, like a giant size detergent. And once a week,
half way down the main road this old man gets on, with a pipe
full of herbal mixture, and that's worse than the hair cream.
He has a little cloth bag full of green stuff he's picked up for
his rabbits I suppose. And he sits at the back near where I sit,
and puffs away at this, oh it's so sweet, herbal stuff from a
long curly pipe. I think he's a retired bench-hand from an
engineering firm, but I'm not sure. I hate pipe-smokers on
early morning buses. It annoys me. I pay my fourpence single.
I am kind to the Caribbean conductor. He's often the only
bloke in the whole bus who doesn't smell. I keep my ticket all
the way down, in case an inspector gets on and asks on
demand for my yellow square though this has never
happened. I refrain from spitting. I have no dog to keep off

the seats. And I get off at the stop right in the centre. At the stop before mine there's usually two or three gets off, and then as soon as the bus starts up for the last flip in, the whole top deck gets up. I try to be first. It's like the rising of the dead. Soon as we move for the last flip, everyone, just everyone stops the coughing and talking, and rises and makes for the stair. I like to be one of the first for if I don't get off quick and make my way I stand a chance of being late. I walk through the centre of the town, and buy a ten of Parks at the paper shop. The faces are always the same — the two old women who chatter away as I pass the picture house, this lovely bird who smiles at me every morning as I pass the Fish Market — she's got lovely legs. The only new ones are the navvies. The Irish labourers wait on the market square for the coaches to take them off to out of town sites and every morning it's a different set of navvies. I turn up at the factory and say a few how do's, and morning, and sometimes a quip about the weather, and I'm there. Times I'll buy a *Herald* as well as my Parks, if I feel I can face reading down there.

I walk up the stairs, and I put my brown day work card in the I B M slot. A bell rings and it's marked with the time on the clock. I've never been late for a weekday yet; but never more than a few minutes early. Always just on 7:27, or 29, or 31 — never 26 or 34. There is a three-minute allowance up to 7:33 for time. I begrudge the firm the extra if I clock in before 7:30. It puts me off for the rest of the day. It isn't that I work the extra two minutes or so, but I'm there all the same; tied to their work schedule, tied down. I go down the stairs to my machine, and turn on the steam. I put on my apron. I'll hang around till about twenty to eight waiting for the steam to come up to the right temperature. I work in a declining industry, and I like that. There's no fear of redundancy, or short time. No pressure to do overtime. No boom and slump. There is just a gradual fall off in staff coming in. It's a small factory. Ought to have been condemned years ago. The bosses come in about half past eight, and by then I shall have turned out a good five dozen or more. When I first came it took me five minutes to do one skin, but now I can do one in a minute, if I want. You soon pick up the easy way of getting through and after that there's nothing more to know.

I work pretty steady from twenty to eight until about a quarter past eight. Then I go out to the lavatory. I turn my apron round to my back side and sit down on the seat to have a few draws, about half a fag, and then I clip the thing and come back to my machine. About nine I put a few tea leaves in a cup and take it out to the boiling water urn and fill it up, and while it cools aside of the machine I do a bit more. At nine-fifteen the buzzer goes for the tea break. It's right above my head. Makes hell of a noise. Then I stop and take out my pack up, and eat my three sandwiches, and drink my tea. After seven minutes a warning buzzer goes. But I take no notice of that. If I did I wouldn't be able to finish my pack up. Then at nine-twenty-five the buzzer for the end of the break goes. I take out my cup and swill it clean, and throw the paper from my pack up into the bin, and I've started again at the machine by nine-twenty-seven. If you take any longer they start to moan. You're supposed to start again on the dot. That's why they have this warning buzzer three minutes before the real end of the break. But they can't say anything, really. I work pretty solid now. It's my best time till about half past ten. Then I go out for a few more draws down the back. Finish my clip. Then I go back till twelve. Sometimes there's a break when I have to go off and fetch some more work, but they like the work to be brought to you. But usually it's on my feet, working this machine right through bar this one trip out to the lav from the end of the tea break to twelve. Along and back goes this roller, each sheet or skin printed in 45–60 seconds by four or five strips. About sixty an hour, clang, clang. Ever so rare I have to change my printing plate, the plate at the bottom that the roller presses the skin onto to make the pattern. This makes a break of about ten minutes, but they don't like you having to do this. They forget it's the only way I'll ever learn the difference between one pattern and another. But they try to keep me on the same plate for as long as they can, and then if it has to be changed just before I go off so I waste less time, with no waiting to find the new temperature for the new plate. This plate it makes little dots, quite pretty really if you look at them close. There's other plates that make fake morocco,* and fake crocodile, and pearl and peccary* and things like that. Goes into wallets and purses and handbags and small leather goods, some of them high class. About five to twelve I give up for the morning. I turn off the steam, and then go out for a pee, and then put my coat on and up the stairs and join the queue, at the clock. I'm usually about half way down the queue so I can't leave off that early. There's always some there before me.

I get hour and a quarter for dinner. I walk up into the town and over the square and I go into this pub. I like a glass of beer

---

* Forms of printing on leather.

at dinner. And there's another point. On what they pay you, you can't afford dinner other than what you get down the railway canteen or at transport unless you can go home and have got a home to go to; and they don't cook none too good at the railway canteen or over at the transport. Well, they can't at a three course for half a crown. I'm funny that way over food. When I eat I like to eat good. I've had at times to do without eating proper so it don't do me no harm missing dinner. I get a meal at night. I'll have a tuppenny packet of nuts or a cob if I'm really hungry at the pub. Only I usually get a cob on Wednesdays when there's the market. They cost ninepence at the pub. Can't really run to that. They're only a tanner on the market. I'll take my time over my pint. I like a pint. It helps to get rid of the dust from the factory. Makes me feel better too. Sometimes I'll play a record on the juke box. I like that one *Halfway to Paradise*. All about how this boy and his girl are good friends but the fellow thinks they ought to be more than friends, after all being friends isn't what he wants. He wants to be in a bit of paradise. It's a good record. Wonderful how they work these words all around one little idea you can put down in a four-letter word. But there's some good records these days, bloody good — Nat King Cole and Gene Vincent. I think he's about one of the best. I'll smoke a couple of fags in the pub, but the dinner break, it's soon gone. If it's fine I'll go out of the pub at about ten to one, and go into this little park they've got. It's a nice little park. Lean my head against this stone wall and sit on the grass and let the sun come down on to my face and my arms and my neck. Sit down and look at the sky, or the trees or listen to the sounds of the town, or look at this statue they've got. I like statues.

It's modern. A woman all in breasts and arse. I like it. It isn't
that it means something. It's just that it's good to look at.
Gives you something to think about, and it's cool and refresh-
ing and yet fits in with the sounds of the town. It's a part of
things, and yet it's set apart, to brood over. I'll read my *Herald*
if I've bought one. But it's the feeling of the beer inside me,
and the sun coming down on me that I like best of all. About
five past one I'll get up and take a slow stroll back.

I get back about one-thirteen. It's the same as the morning.
I work to tea break with just half a clip out the back at about
two. Then at three the buzzer goes and I have a cup of tea and
an apple. I like apples. The tea break's from three to ten past.
Then work from then to twenty-five past five with just one
break out the back. Join the last queue. Wait for the last
buzzer. And then it's another day gone. On Monday you get
that Monday feeling. Worst day is Thursday. Then on Friday
you can't pass the time too quick for that pay packet and the
last buzzer of the week. But you push on. It gets mechanical
after a time, like you stop living and go all half dead. Five
days a week. You stand at your machine and sing and think
and talk to yourself just to pass the time. You can't concen-
trate. I have never been absent. I am a good worker, well fair.
I can't be that bad because they pay me a bit over what they
would because I've stuck at the job. There's no one to boss me
around like there has been at other places. There's no sense of
urgency, or boom, or decline. It's pretty steady. You know the
next day will be much like the one before. You get into a routine. You have to. You never really notice it's a declining
industry. That's only what they show in the annual returns, or
when you look through the order books for three years ago,

or the carriers' books for the goods going out. If I stay on a bit longer I'll go on piece-work. Then it'll have to be over 100 an hour, not a mere 60. It wouldn't pay you else. I don't know if I've got the know-how, and what it takes to go on piece-work. You've got to be fast, really fast. One daydream and you're lost. I take out Fridays always over eight. It's not bad really. I'm just under five bob an hour. It's a flat week, no overtime. The tax and all that hits me a bit bad because I'm single. Statistically I'm earning around ten a week, but I never see that. That's better than the basic rate of just about nine a week. I can't really grumble because I've come here while I was down, but I could. I could grumble, but where's the use? And so I don't really fancy changing my brown day card for a white piece-worker's card. You can earn over fourteen on piece work, even in take home pay, but they make sure you sweat blood for it. Of course you have to if you've got kids. There's no other chance. I think I earn my money. I suppose it's what they call a fair week's pay for a fair week's work. I pay two pound for my board and the rest's mine. And all the rest of the time too, though all but at weekends you're tied down to that clock. I stay in most nights, go round the local about nine for just a pint. Drink by myself in the corner. Don't say nothing. At weekends I take a coach away to where we've got this little flat. I stay over Saturday night. Might get married. I save about four pound a week. It all adds up. You see I don't eat except at nights and that's covered by my board. I don't drink a lot—two pints a day, and a bottle of whisky now and then. I don't smoke a lot—just over ten a day. I don't gamble, or go out dancing. If I go to the cinema I take the cheapest seats. I lead a quiet life. I haven't got any friends, not here, and I don't really want any. I'm content, I suppose, in my way.

You don't love your job?

No. I have no interest. It is just a job. I need the money. I might have had an interest, but they killed that. All the interest, all the variety, all that could give me an interest in their leather, they keep all that to themselves strictly within the family. They made me just a worker. I don't work for them. I work at their factory, and I hate it.

You wanted to do something else?

No, nothing definite. Not really. You see I drifted around a great deal after I left school, from job to job and town to town. It took me a long time to settle down. I've come to terms alright now.

Have you?

No, but don't you see if I stayed at that factory for about a year all the fight and go and guts, they would disappear; and what would be left of me would be a shell.

You're in love?

Not really, and not like that. The weekend, it's the only time I ever really talk; the only friend I have.

But of course you're a little different. You have a sensitive nature.

No, that it isn't it. The way I feel about work at that place is the same as most of them feel, only after you've been there a bit you lose the ability to express it; your wit gets deadened. You know the words, but can't get them out. This has got nothing to do with sensitive nature, the poor artist having to graft in a factory. It's the factory and the way they run it and not in me that the fault lies.

You would go off balance if anything happened over the weekends? Yes, I would. But I think I'd get over it. I wouldn't lose any time at work. I have a routine now. It's satisfying, and has made me come to terms. You can't have what you want can you? My life is pretty well mechanical now. I've got a rhythm. Maybe it isn't a rhythm of life. Fact, I know it's the rhythm of the factory ingrained into my own system but it stops me having to think. I have no deep emotions, and no thoughts about myself any more. If anything happened I could carry on by instinct more than anything else. I have left behind my friends, my hopes, desires, dreams. I have consciously lost them. I am content now, in a way. There are no promotions, no overtime, no rat race, no foreman, no status symbols, no keeping up with the others. I have come to terms, but it isn't with life. It's with the factory. I am quite happy, or I can kid myself that I am. In a way quite pleased with the life I have.

You are?

Yes, I am.

Yet you dream of other things?

What seems now a long time ago, almost as if it was a part of me that I've since lost, I did dream.

And now you say you have none?

Look, have you ever done continuous graft? Until you find a routine, until you come to terms with what is, and not what might be or could be, but what is in the factory then the graft is unbearable. Until you become numb, until you cease to think, until you subordinate yourself to the factory, working is very, very painful. There's nothing wrong with this subordination in itself. It's just that as it is now it cuts out a whole chunk of the you, of your life, personality. It doesn't give you a chance.

A long time ago, well it seems a long time ago I wanted to be physically free, to lead the charmed life. I went from job to job searching, looking for some pattern some way in which I could build up a life in the way I wanted: to work hard and fully and make use of imagination and guts and a love of life, and yet not be tied down; be free to come and go, not in the job itself but to be able to know that after two years there would be a break and then another different job; a job where I could make use of myself. But then there were the down bits. Have you ever been unemployed? Walk down the streets, wait for the first editions of the papers. You must have money. You get too gutless to steal. You get too proud to take the National Assistance or the Benefit. You take it in the end, but so reluctantly. And you have no money. Everyone else is in work of some kind. Everyone else has money. When you've had bits of down like this time and time again, and then when you find that on the up bits you're either in bad luck, or you can't turn out right, you arrive at this point, this point of giving up when someone comes along and offers you a job, an ordinary killing steady job like the one I've got. And you say to yourself I hate this job, but it's a job and it stops the ache of the search for the pattern you want. And so I shall stick to this job until I have come to terms with it, and have killed any aspirations for something I really wanted. It isn't that bad, you kid yourself. You want it. You cling to it. You're in a warm cell and the life is bearable, and there are little compensations, and you remember the outside, the struggle of finding your own way, the really hard twenty-four-hour work, and the two jobs to get through, and the bits of poverty and unemployment. And so you stick, and the little compensations become the life, and the real fades away. No, once I dreamt of being physically free. Not now. I have come to terms, I kid myself. I have a certain peace, a certain security. It's not that I'm afraid of losing my job. I'm scared stiff of losing my attitude, my coming to terms, my defeat, scared of losing that. I'm on my own again, if all this goes. I took that for a long time. I don't think I could take it again, any road I'm not going to try. I kid myself. So I stick to my job at the factory where I work. I go respectable and law abiding and can't bear the ones who still struggle on to find a way. I don't want to lose the little I have. It holds me together. Don't talk revolution or rebellion. I want to keep my little.

You don't dream any more?

Yes, I have my dreams but I try not to let on. I still dream. If you've ever done continuous graft you'll know what I mean. We all dream — the pools, the horses, the book, the song. Why is it that people think there's something wrong in dreaming, something wrong in wanting to win the pools? You stand at that bloody machine and hum and sing and dream and dream and dream. And you can never tell anyone what you really dream of. You daredn't, for fear it would stop you coming to terms, the little compensation you have. Until after a time you can't even put the dreams into words.

I come out of the factory at half past five and I walk across the town to the bus terminus. The other day someone stopped me, someone I hadn't seen for two years. He said — grafting now. I said, how can you tell. I wasn't wearing clothes any different from those I normally wear. He said he could smell the graft on me, and the look of me mouth and me eyes. I can take the graft. I can do it. But I can't stop the graft from making deadpan lines on my face, lines not of struggle but of passive acceptance. Lines with the fight and the guts gone out. When I see this old bloke in the bus queue before me. He works at our place. His mouth is open and his eyes just stare, all open and he droops over the rail. Christ, don't let me die like that.

Yes, I dream, dream of being free from having to work at a job I have no joy in, work just to keep myself alive. I dream of being free, physically. I dream of writing and reading and wandering all over meeting people and talking — there's nothing concrete there. Nothing, I can say I am going to work at until I have made this dream come true. It's just a dream. Like most people I have only a glimmering of how to put this into practice. I just want to be free, more than anything else.

Once I had a job that took every hour of my time. It was a job I loved. It was something I could go into 100 per cent, and still come up for more. Yet I couldn't take it. I never had to fight for it. It was offered me on a plate, on my terms. It was like winning the pools. You've dreamt about it for so long that when it comes you don't know quite what to do with it, not the money but the freedom. That was the strangest thing about that whole affair. Working in a factory I thought I was alright and sound in self-discipline and all that. Particularly in the simple physical things like getting up in time for work, working for hour-long stretches, having a good time away from the factory but never to the point where being at the factory in the morning is forgotten. And not working Saturday or Sunday overtime to the point where you have to take Monday off to get over it. I thought I was alright. I thought I had enough physical control over what I was doing with my time. I thought this physical discipline was my own self-discipline. That's one of the dreadful things about working in a factory. You take a pride in the rational way you run your life. But in fact it's not you, but the factory that has the control. All the time at the factory, at home and out; all the time with the possible exception of Saturday night and Sunday morning your physical control is that of the factory. When the factory goes, when you leave and are out on your own the control goes. When the dream comes true the old checks and balances that you thought of as yours, they go; because they never really belonged to you. They were a part of the factory. There becomes no leisure time. Work and home and out get fused. We are still hopelessly equipped for looking after ourselves. I just didn't know what to do with my time in the physical sense. I was only equipped for work and play. When the two came together, when the dream came true I was lost.

It's interesting how many writers in particular from ordinary backgrounds do two jobs — movie management and drama; magazine editor and creative writing, and the old one of lecturer or teacher with writing. The two parts are linked but the idea of work and leisure is still kept to some extent. It's funny. I stopped writing apart from articles as soon as I took my job at Leicester, and it's only now that I've left that I've taken up again. If I ever get handed the plate again, with this dream of working in or with something I want to do, something I'm passionately interested in I don't think I'll make the same mistakes. But if I don't make the mistakes again it will be because of learning that this dream of a fusion between work and leisure can't quite work out.

Work, nine hours a day in the factory. I hate it, in a way. Yet in another I like it. It restores the balance. I know where I am. It gives me free time. But it kills you, because the factory becomes the centre of your life and not the you.

Ah, I mustn't kid myself. I'll be gone from here soon enough. The itch in my feet that I can't stop, it'll get me again, and I'll be off. I stand up on this stage talking to myself.

Look out, look out into the auditorium and I see that it's empty, but for You. There are no longer any blue or white spotlights focused on me. The electricians have gone home. But I can see You. You sit in a seat at the back. You look bored. You look as if you were waiting for me to stop talking, and You have waited a long while.

Alright. Walk down the steps and along the gangway. I look at You, and we smile. I see your brown eyes, and your black hair, and your white skin. I move towards You, to touch You. I love You. I put out my hand, but there is nothing there, nothing.

Once I was very tired. I had walked a long way. I had a job getting lifts. I got to Towcester at three in the morning, a Sunday morning. It was cold and misty. There was no traffic. There was a telephone kiosk lit up, and people kept waiting for someone to finish a phone conversation. There was a long queue. I watched them as I sat on a kerbstone until it was dawn, and when dawn came there was nobody there at all. Funny, the things you see when you're tired, very tired.

eleven

BACK ON THE ROAD, DOWN TOWARDS LONDON. LONDON.
And from London out through the suburbs from Victoria, to
the no man's land, Surrey, Tennessee Williams country; the
power stations at Hackbridge, scrub, beech trees, bushes,
backs of a seedy suburbia, factories; the trollies at Mitcham,
rubbish heaps and bonfires, a stream and an olde worlde
bridge; posters for the West End show, new flats, Tudor
imitation, semi-detached; the intricate map on the compartment wall, the plaque — Lacewood England — coming out of
the station, past the Magnolia School of Dancing, the names
of the houses, St. Helier Jersey, the honeymoon resort, the
1939 shop sets, and then the great Gothic mental hospital anno
domini 1853 opposite a row of prefabs and a railway line in
the valley. Out to see a friend and then back through this
much-charted country. Like Africa and youth it's been almost
hacked to death, and yet there's still something more to read,
something more to comment on.

> Wet or fine we will take the Brighton line; we will fly
> From this city of cats, coal black in business hats
> To the now, where we can lie, even die,
> Brown and blue in a sea-sand cyclone of sin,
> Happy and hay hampered in a shimmering cell
> Of white beer bubbly bliss.

And the waves will wash the waning shore,
Whimpering in a gush of wet on the slipping sand,
Till we have had our fill of rock, races, seashow and sense.
Then lurching late in dim lusty teak
We will lullabye back to the pepsi peopled pollution.

As still from a high convent wall a girl softly sang of a man
On a tree, yellow water, lollipopped in laughing
    blood-filled pus.
She sang of a God on a stick and she sang it for us.

Once there were points of reference: religion, politics, dreams; but now there are none. I see what I see. I hear what I hear. Then I move on. Like an observer I just look, but biased, partial. I look with and through my own eyes, not quite straight. The way I want to look. And what were once points of reference are now a way of life, a backcloth I myself take for granted, and don't have to refer to. I know it's there, and I leave it at that.

But once, I had to refer to it, make sure of myself, keep reminding myself of where I had consciously decided to take my stand. And in doing so the picture was neither honest to myself or honest to the idea.

Worthing and The Dome. An amusement arcade on the pier. A penny lost in the slot to determine the day's fortune. The reading of the tea leaves. I feel a sense of belonging, a sense of security down there in The Dome. I can see what I want to see. There I have the stuff for dreams, and thoughts and feelings; points of contact, points from which I can soar away off on my own. I like The Dome, and the Pier and the Front. I like that part of the Coast.

But there is more to the Coast than that. There is religion, good citizens, decent folk, the caring, the old, the past glory, the idea of a society where we all help one another. Where us the charmed and chosen, us the superior can enjoy ourselves and assert our superiority by handing out the chocolate-coated crumbs to the lower orders. Lunch at Mitchells. A lady. Large, sending her rice back — all milk and no grains. India. Husband a Brigadier, brother a colonel, and friends out there. The owner was the Mayor once, a good Christian man although a little bit middle class. Nothing in flying. India next week. Well, my husband was out there for thirty years. Live with one of my maids now, and an Alsatian. Tea at Warnes is very good. I used to give 1/– tip there. Well, off now — change a book at Boots, and then the Red Cross. Marry again? Couldn't. The great divide. Couldn't put anybody in his place. We shall meet on the other side, my husband and I. Good afternoon. It has been nice meeting you.

I like Worthing, I can sit in The Dome by the juke box and watch my duty pass by through the plate-glass window, watch it die. I can walk along the front and watch my heritage wheeled out of Warnes for its last breath of the sleepy Worthing air.

But all this is wrong. Warnes and India and lunch at Mitchells, this isn't my heritage. MacWonder* making his Edwardian promises, he doesn't talk about the England I belong to. I don't hate you. You're just irrelevant. Ivanhoe charging on a white steed through the fields of Buckinghamshire right into our little home, this isn't England. When I walk past the newsboards and see 'Our

---

* Harold Macmillan, British Prime Minister 1957–1963.

Marines Moved In'; 'Our Men Flown Out', it doesn't move me. It doesn't register. It doesn't mean a thing. It is irrelevant and pointless.

Yet it isn't. It's all so bloody true. You can't laugh it off. The *Sunday Express* falls on the doormat. And that isn't all. It isn't MacWonder the Music Hall man, it's all the gobblers, all the Butlers and MacLeods and Gaitskells, not being shocked but taking it all in, and appointing spokesmen — the Queen's representative of the lower orders, the gimmicky ever so funny little man who's such a delightful rebel, you must hear him, he's so ever so funny.

And we play right into their hands. Either we believe them and give in and go all nice and make our tracks on that outward bound course to the OBE. Or, and this is worse, we retreat to The Dome and say that we love it because it's so nasty and seedy and so much being the rebel and going against all of them. And that gives them everything. They can say, look at him in that caff, it's ever so funny. We must be tolerant and let him work it out, help him to work it out and still go our own way. And so they leave us to The Dome and the seedy and the raffshness and they know as we don't that we'll either succumb or we'll be just the same as the folks at Warnes, dying away slowly and rather interestingly but without any importance or any significance.

I like Worthing, but it isn't good for me. It doesn't get anywhere. Whether I go down to The Dome and scream out look at me; or go to Warnes and scream at them it will have no importance. It may be funny, but it won't matter. Back to London, by road. Through the night. Coffee by the stall at King's Cross. Another passage of time. Off again. Wandering around, looking, just looking and making notes and then moving on; quickly before they put a label on me and slot me into a charming every so funny little pigeon-hole.

We had come from London by train and by boat. Drunk Leopold in a second class direct. They told us the autostrad from Oostende was the fastest road in Europe, but we hadn't got a car. Belgium was much the same. On Friday we saw King B. of the B's.* We saw white cars police; a man in a Cadillac with an envelope. The guard at the palace was chewing gum and wearing dark glasses. We wished we had brought our camera. The clubs were much the same — Parisiana, Lido, Strip Tease, Follies, London, Miami — reflecting an interest in geography, and demonstrating the mobility of sex. A police cadet took us round the suburbs. They were much the same as Nottingham. The bars were better. The records on the juke boxes were much the same. We missed the Caribbeans. We sat in a flat we got invited into looking over on to the Grand Place and watched some carnival, while we talked of the Walloons,** and the problem in a broken French and a broken English. We made out alright. I went to the Flemish parts on my own and got lost, and nobody understood what I was saying, which isn't unusual except that I began to wonder if I understood myself what I was trying to say. Went back to these intellectuals over the Grand Place. They thought we were rather naive, and a little misguided but it wasn't because we were young. There is a strip of water between our island and the Continent. They told us this. We believed them, but they still smiled. I told them that there was a strip of land between Saint Albans and

---

* King Bandouin of Belgium, 1951–1993.

** French-speaking Belgians.

Northampton that divided the dead from the living. They hadn't heard of Northampton. I told them that not everyone who lived in Britain was a Britisher; that there were many millions of Englishmen living in Britain. They didn't believe me. The licensing laws were a blessing.

We took the T.E.E. to Paris. The railway stations at Brussels were alright and more. We liked the Central best. There were escalators from the precinct to the platforms, and the train was good. There were green poplars and electric cooling towers, and the countryside was flat. We drank Weils Pils and looked out at thin Common Market cows. There were rubbish dumps and prefabs and houses coloured red and orange, and new blocks of flats, and then there was getting off the train and changing our currency. The man at the Bureau de Change said in English — these will do for the juke box. We bought an English magazine and took coffee in a café opposite. We sat on a terrace and got the coffee all mixed up, and changed to beer. There was an article in this English magazine saying that France was now more like a South American republic than a great European nation. As neither of us had been to South America we couldn't comment. France looked much the same to me. There was a heavy hand on my shoulder. I thought it was going to start up all over again — the police and the questions, and the sitting in the car to the Embassy and the talk and the moralizing and the flight back and the talk from the London police and then my long letters and please, and paying backs before my passport would be returned — but it wasn't. It was a man we met before. Well, well, Thursday I see you Rotterdam, Sunday I see you

---

* Trans-Europ Express.

Bruges, Tuesday I see you Brussels and now I see you here. We had a chat, and passed on a tip about a wonderful chicken place just at the back of the Gare Du Midi in Brussels. He said he had to be back Hamburg by next week, and we told him we had to be back Nottingham as soon as we could. We stayed in Paris for a little while. There were a few friends to look up and a few places to go to again. Paris was just the same. And then there was coming back by train, missing the fast and having to take the slow — Amiens, Arras, Lens, Bethune, Dunkerque, London and stopping at Bedford and it was just the same. Urchins giving the V sign and shouting obscenities, and a large notice explaining Modernization Schemes now in progress.

We had travelled across Europe and England, and I had moved away from where I had been brought up and out to take my stand waiting for a tramcar beneath the Gare du Nord; waiting and watching and looking; taking the stand from the start, from the side of the Worthing Dome. That was my point of departure. When all the past, all the things that happened that weren't all my own doing had been added up. When I had reached a sum total for the past, and could move on in my own way on my own conscious path.

That was my point of departure, my own personal point of departure where the past got tied up and the present became the all important, the Dome at Worthing, a point of departure I could start from, not upwards, or downwards but across in my own pattern.

After moving away from Them, and being determined not to be a part of the real Worthing; not to die like that in a wheelchair on the veranda at Warnes, there came the determination to start from The Dome. Somewhere to start from and move away from in one's own pattern as soon as possible.

And to leave behind the way they'd like to see us; ever so nasty and funny and raffish and poor and humble and fit only to be shut away in one little caff on the Front at Worthing.

And to leave behind the way they'd like to see us; moving into their world as equal partners in theory (except they've had centuries of experience and we've had none) in their little game of keeping the two worlds apart — isn't he funny, take him in, just like the real thing only he has a sense of humour, and can sing and write and things, take him in, foster him and he'll change, and forget the rest.

No, I belong down there and I stay down there; but if I need the moon and you stand in my way I shall fight for the moon, because if I need the moon I have a right to the moon.

No, I stay for me and us and now and our life and my life and stay to see it doesn't get crapped up, or bogged down, or uplifted into the deadwood that dinksies about at the top of the trees.

No, I stay on the ground, and it isn't a down there. It's the most wonderful, the only life I know, enjoy, need, and ever want to know.

No, I stay and this is just a beginning. I've added up the past, and now I make a start, the real start from the ground.

That's how Leicester began. And Leicester showed me how difficult it is. And Leicester showed me where I was good, and where I was weak and least happy. And then when Leicester was all over, and I could look back. It showed me because of what happened, and not in spite of what happened, that I know I was right then, and am so now; not that I as a person am right, but that I've got my feet on the right side, and that's what really is important.

twelve

YES, AND THEN THERE WAS LEICESTER. IN A WAY IT'S
still a city I love more than any other, and not just because of
what happened, what I did; not just because I have friends,
memories. Leicester is very English, and Provincial English in
the best sense. It's a city that grows on you, if you ever live
in it. It's no El Dorado, like Coventry. It's solid, and this
makes it appear to the visitor, to me when I go back, like an
hostile town. It's not. It's just that it's a closed place, a solid
community. You live in it. For a bit you hate it, and then
slowly when you go to other places you realise it's grown on
you. You miss it. You get proud that you come from there,
quietly proud. You miss it.

The first time I can ever remember coming to Leicester
was one winter. I was hitching south from Nottingham to
London, and it was snowing — that snow sleet drizzle rain
stuff that seems to climb down from the skies. It was a very
dark night, and I was dropped on the northern outskirts at
about three in the morning. I followed the route signs and
moved slowly through this stuff that was coming down
towards the centre. There wasn't a light on anywhere. I only
saw one person the whole way in, and that was this kid. It was
funny this. I saw him that first night all alone, with his coat
collar up, Italian suit, no raincoat, no hat, battering his way

through the sleet out of town as I was coming in. I saw him at the first dances we ran. I saw him down at the club. I saw him on the afternoon I left. I saw him on the morning I went out of Leicester, as I was crossing to the station he was coming out. I've seen him since. I know his name now, but it's funny that. The first person I saw in Leicester, and I keep on seeing him; as I pass through in a car, or as I cross stations.

I got to the coffee stall and Old Don fixed me up with a coffee, and said he'd do his best to find me a truck ride south, but after an hour of hanging around I moved off to the London Road to have a go at getting a lift on my own. I stood on the corner, and remember this great big cleaning van calling at this shop, loading up and unloading and then moving off again.

And then this D* car pulls up beside me. Two D men get out and one of them starts questioning me—Who are you? Where you going? What's in the bag? Got any proof? I kept looking into the cop car and there sitting beside the driver was a man with a trilby and a short moustache, smiling all wry, and giving me the look over. That's another face I keep seeing, every time I go through that place, even now. I tell you, Jamo, I tell you this that even if you and I had both known all of what would happen, you wouldn't have been able to stop me. I remember you saying to me once, when I was up at the station over something when we were running the club. You said to me—Ray, you're wrong, you're so wrong. Well, I tell you this. It's all over now, and I've been through the hard stuff. Maybe I didn't go inside, but I never

* Detective.

had it easy after I left. I've been through the hard and now I'm free and on top again, and I can laugh and look back and with no regrets. I know you're a good copper, and you're alright; but I still believe like I believed then, and I still say to you what I said to you then—I can't be of no use to you. I wouldn't ever tell you nothing. I don't *reckon* I was right. I know I was right. Last time I passed you I was coming out of the Fountain, and you looked at me and laughed. Well, I can laugh back at you. Don't worry. You're a good copper. By the time I got to that station and got quizzed by you lot, Leicester had bitten me. I was going to come back. It wasn't a town like Northampton, and it wasn't a big open city like Nottingham. It was large enough to be manageable, and yet not big enough to get lost in'.

Next time I came into Leicester was for an interview at the University. It was snowing then, with real big flakes. Again I hitched in, and I was wet. I got put off at the railway station and asked people where the University was. Never knew there was one. Go down this street, and then left, and you'll see it on your right-hand side.

I did. It was the Art and Tec. I tried again. Did anyone know where the University was?

No, but someone knew where a University Road was.

I found that. Walked along it, and saw this great big impressive building. Must be the University. Walked across the snow up to the front door.

No Sir, this is the grammar school for girls. Try along the road.

I did. I found the prison. I went back. Tried along the other turning. Found this funny building opposite a cemetery. It really did look like the mental hospital it was before it got taken over. It was in the days before all the new extensions. Found a porter. Got showed up to an office. Queued up. Step inside.

You look very wet. Come far?

Across the border.

You must be very tired. Did you travel overnight?

No, I motored in.

Dear, dear — looks at the forms in front of him and sees that I came from Northampton. Oh, yes, the border, Northampton. I thought you meant Scotland.

No, the county border, and it really is a border, a great divide.

We talked about Larkin and Silkin, Amis and Gunn; and then I left, and I went down the stairs into the students' part. At that time it was a Crush room where the cloakrooms are now. I opened the door, and went in, and there were people talking away, clouds of smoke, music, jeans, suéde jackets and black stockings, and Southern accents and laughter haa haa hee hee. I wasn't staying there.

I went out and into the Town. I tried to find a juke box caff, something I knew, some little part of my own country. I couldn't find one. Had an egg and chips somewhere, and went into a pub after. It was all old old working class with no lads, no juke box, and no old gels. Found a cinema. They were showing Presley's *Jailhouse Rock*. I went in on my own, and came out with my own bird tagging on my arm. Said good-bye, by the bus-stop, and promised to come over again. I don't know who they were. I don't think I've ever seen them again, but it was alright. I went back to Northampton.

Leicester's alright, University or no University. I like Leicester. Few weeks later they offered me a place at the University, and I accepted.

And then the first day at the University, and I came in with the sun on an afternoon coach and parked myself at the south end of the town, where the University hostels were. I'd got off the coach with two large cases, and they were both heavy. I took one of the cases across the road, and asked this road-mending team if they'd mind looking after it till I found where to dump the first case. They said they didn't mind. Just looked a little shocked. I took the other case along the road and into the hostel, and found my room. There were four beds, all single. Only one was in a corner. I put my case on the corner bed, opened it and filled enough drawers beside it to show that I had taken possession, that I had moved in to stay, for better or worse. I locked the case, and went back to the roadmen's hut to collect the second case. It was still there.

By the time I got back to my room there was another — tennis, men's wear, Chelmsford, Geography something, motor-cycle, quiet, assured.

No, please, please.

The second arrived — men's wear pre-war vintage, Mathematics something, Chipping Ongar, greased, curly hair, nervous.

Then number three — Haslemere, strange, men's wear, but with the touch — my own personal cravat only I don't like to call it a cravat — he laughed. Made a change. Brought books with him, and not just text-book stuff, but real living books.

But they all had certain qualities in common, like pale pimply faces, black toe-capped shoes, heavily greased hair laid down flat with parting. They were all obviously and painfully poor, and meek all through. The poverty of the middle-classes, and the nervous inhibitions. The beds were— well, the only other place I'd seen beds like them was in a Surrey mental hospital, State-controlled before modernisation. There were no carpets on the floor, but a polished wood, the nasty, much too clean-smelling sort. It was charming, a real charmer. I had a small window at the side of my bed, the privilege of the corner, and from this window I could see one tree. I remember my first words to the first another.

I'm Ray, call me Ray. What you call yourself?

The reply went purple in the face. Not red, but purple and said I'm ...

I've forgotten his name. There was a silence. Then I said.

Wonderful weather.

Yes, it is nice today.

And that bit is verbatim, monosyllabic.

Now, the whole point was that I had made a great effort to integrate myself, not to cause a stir, or seem out of place. I wanted to be unaggressive, cut out the arrogance, cut out the localised accents, the harshness. I was willing and determined to make great sacrifices to fit into the life of this Universitette. I really did. I'd a white shortie mack on, a black suit, a crisp white shirt, a nice blue tie. I must have smelt faintly of after-shave lotion, and most important of all was that morning I'd been to see Reggie, my barber, and got him to cut off my hair and do something suitable for my new job. Well, what Reggie thought suitable wasn't, it seemed, any good. It was sort of lacquered with no hair cream into a sort of Tony Curtis, all light and well razored and just lifting above the head. I stayed in that place with the others till around seven o'clock, and then I gave up. Took a bus into the University proper, to the students' part.

I went into the students' bar and it was full, very full, and all across one half of the room sat groups of students much older than myself. They all seemed to have come from London and the south, and they all wore variations on men's wear, and they sang a song, 'I don't know who you are Sir, or where you're from but you've done me a power of go-o-od'. They leant back on their metal, modern chairs, all cold, and back slappish and cheery and ruggery. It seemed vulgar and all out of place. The right song but with the wrong people in the wrong place. And all I wanted was a quiet drink and to slowly get the feel of the place. There was no chance to do this. The feel of the place came across not in the smoke and atmosphere, but it was pushed at you. There was nothing there, tangible and warm waiting for me to touch. It was pushed at me. Join in with us or get out, you slob. There seemed nowhere to sit, but with them. And they kept singing that song and laughing, heartily laughing with all the throat and none of the guts. I stood at the bar and finished my drink as quickly as I could and went out of the building and across the road and along by the cemetery wall and slowly into the town. I found a pub, the first bar I came to, on the main street, and I went in to the back room and took a seat and a drink and although this wasn't a bar I'd have chosen for myself, I was at ease again.

There were many groups in the pub, but I wasn't over-powered. There was an equality, and ordinariness. I could be anonymous, and sit in my corner and be left alone. I was out of the wedding party I hadn't been invited to, and I was back in a real public institution. But the song, that song still remained. I still sing it to myself, quite often. It was such a wonderful song.

Somehow it's got linked up with the first time I went to Brussels, as a contrast. It was '58, the year of the International Exhibition. I was in a bar along by the Expo Park and there were coaches on the park outside from Warsaw and Belgrade, Paris and Berlin, Madrid and London; and the bar room was full, and there was a band, a German band. It was an international occasion, and the barriers were down and they made you join in and if you wouldn't they forgot you. Without any more to it, they forgot you. I remember dancing round and round with a little Bavarian woman and everyone got tipsy on the atmosphere rather than the beer and spirits. It was so different from that students' place, and yet it needn't have been. There was no sense of a closed group. The bar-room was wide open, and I felt like I belonged to the whole world and the whole world belonged to me. I remember that song. It brings together a place where I felt free and happy and warm and alive; and that student bar where I felt so shut in I either had to go away, or smash the tables and stop that song—'I don't know who you are Sir, or where you're from, but you've done me a power of go-o-od'. I hated that place.

Why? Why?

They were nearly all southerners, conscious, superior, real south of Saint Albans. Most of them were either nice men's wear, poor middle classy or, worse, very consciously working class, with the sort of consciousness that comes from never having belonged or having rejected and yet regretting the rejection, regretting it all very much. I could imagine what was in the few cases I knew very true; I could imagine that when they went back to their homes in south or east London, to their family, their streets, town, district, there would be no contact and they regretted this. The sort of rejections that led to the way they were so aggressive about being common, not working class but common, all beatniky and vulgar. No, I couldn't stand that. People who wandered through shouting it at you — I'm common as shit and proud of it, and yet when you broke the barrier down they weren't common as shit at all in any sense. Like the laughter it was just a sound, something throaty without any bowels to it. They had come to the University for the better degree, and the better way of life, and weren't honest enough to admit it. They were all the sort who when the truck driver picks them up from the roadside he says — You're a student, and he knows he's right every time, and that puts an end to any conversation, or else it's student/lorry driver conversation. This, as a contrast to being a kid at a University studying either for a degree, or for just the thing.

But I think more than anything, the one thing that got me was the total lack of curiosity, the complete deadness of any imagination, or awareness. The interest stopped at the syllabus and the social round.

In the hostel most of them worked away at the syllabus; played tennis, drank in the village, took their girl to the central picture house, went home one weekend in four. And anything like the interest in things, and a response to things that I had found in factories, pubs, caffs, on the railway; this just didn't exist. The energy they put into the syllabus had to be seen to be believed; the dedication, the desperate systematic plodding on towards the final examination — it was fantastic. But as far as any idea of what was going on around them, or what was happening to themselves, or any interest even in what they were reading the degree for — no, nothing.

Now this isn't, of course, quite true. There were people I could talk with, people like Taffy. Taffy was a Welshman from Wales with a father who had money. Taffy knew intuitively about things. He was wise. I could come back at three, four of a Sunday morning and find Taffy, sitting up and reading away, the only person often for miles around who was awake, and I could talk and get talk back from then until dawn. I could pour out and he'd listen, and then the talk would come back. Start with Dylan Thomas and go through Socialism and Wales and Ebbw Vale and his own poetry, and Women and Coloureds, and Queers, and Elvis Presley and the Palais and E.M. Forster. Taffy could do this, and he wasn't the only one; take and use and give out the sort of long rambling talks that go on until dawn when completely exhausted one can get to sleep and really sleep. Course, things got a little difficult with the other three in the room. On the first night I came back from the Town at around eleven. I was the only one alive in the whole building, and when I went into the room, there were these three sleeping figures. I thought it was the end of the world. Nix. No future. No charmers. No nowt. There they were asleep, and I wanted to turn on the radio and dance or something and shout and scream, but the whole place was shut, closed, asleeping away.

But it wasn't just the lack of talking. I was out of my country, the world I'd grown to know and love, and I missed it terribly. I missed the front room full of books, my own room, full of books, and paper. I was prepared for the University to be like the front room, like the monastery, and rooms I had known at Oxford and Cambridge and Nottingham, and even London — a room large enough to keep books and bed, and yet small enough to stamp with one's own trademarks. It wasn't like this. There were three others in the room. It was so big. I couldn't shut myself up. It was the first and the last time this ever happened. I missed my own loneliness. And then the Town, the social life. The Students' Union, it was shut up. It was like this big room with four beds and a polished floor. It hadn't got the wide open, the mixture, the contacts, the life and warmth I'd grown to expect.

But even with the compensations, like the wonderful library, and the chance the others didn't get, I had to go away every weekend for the first few months. Then in the midweek. On a week night I'd go out on to the main A6, thumb a lift — stop a driver and say just — look, drive me somewhere will you? Anywhere, wherever you're going — I'd do London and back in a night; or down the Watling Street, to some caff, a tea and then hitch back; or just as far as Harborough. It didn't matter. It was away, talking like I liked to talk, two way; and the radio, the arrogance, the confidence, the juke box, the spontaneous responses; and then back to the hostel — a black coffee and up to the Hall for breakfast and then go to bed, lectures or no lectures. And the char, she'd come in — but Mister Gosling what's the matter? It doesn't matter. It doesn't matter. I'm alright now.

But you need money, even to hitch; and there were times when I didn't have enough even to hitch a ride, well pay for the coffee half way, and that was how the Leicester thing began. It would have begun in any place, but being without money, walking around the streets had got me bitten by the place much faster. I started going in with money, moving from one bar to another, just looking, taking the smell; looking and listening. Getting the feel of the place and then moving on; finding my way around. I made no contacts. I wasn't going to get involved. It was just looking; just looking.

.   .   .

I used to come back to the hostel from the Town on a bus. Now, the hostel was in the posh end; and on the bus there used to be this kid, every other night or so; sharp in a soft sort of way, and he used to have this great big guitar with him, all like a national press cartoon. But there was one thing wrong — the district. Apart from the student hostels there was nothing for miles around but these great big detached houses, one of the largest posh ends in the Midlands. What was this kid doing up at this end of the town?

One night I walks up with this kid, and we gets talking.

What you got the guitar for?

I play it, what you think?

Where you play it then?

In a pub.

What's the name of the pub? He tells me.

What night you play up there then? Mondays.

Mind if I turn up one night? If you want to.

There was one thing that struck me very fierce over this talk. He never asked me where my interest was. This was strange, but never mind.

And then one night, weeks later, I went along to the pub. The first time I sat in the public downstairs and listened to what the regulars said about the band practice, for that was all it was, that was going on upstairs. I watched the band come down for their drinks. It was interesting. Never saw the kid.

Second time I went upstairs, taking a pint with me. I stood at the back of this practice room and listened. No one stopped me, or said owt. They were a good band, really good with a great guitarist and a fabulous drummer. Drank my beer and went out. Said nothing. But the kid, the one from the posh end who carried the guitar, he was the band's leader and vocalist, he must have seen me.

Third time I went to the pub, I took a pint up to the top room and I introduced myself to the singer, the kid with the guitar from the posh end, and I was in. After that I'd drink there pretty regular Monday nights. I liked going there. It was alright. Made a change. If anything turned out it just turned out.

Over the weeks I became a part of the band's feature. To the band itself I was, and to some extent remained, a stranger, a foreigner — suspicious. But to the kid, the singer, I was the Man, a fan with a brain; and to some extent I remained that. It's a pity that. But the element of suspicion and the embarrassments, it was two sided. It was new to me, and I was new to them. This being new and strange dogged the whole of the time through Leicester, both for me and for everyone else; a pity, inevitable, terribly sad.

Come to one of our dates up at working men's club. You can carry the drums in.

And so I did. Alright. Following the band around, a professional friend, a professional observer.

Come to the Palais. We're in the talent competition.

I did. Alright.

And by this time I'd taken over a flat in the centre of the city, along by the prison. And I knew that I wasn't going back to the University for a second year. I was finding the smooth way out without annoying or upsetting anyone too much. You can't just leave. But what was I going to do? I didn't know. Hadn't any idea. Just wander around. Wait. Something'd turn up. I kept on using the pubs, and going around with the band, carrying the drums in at halls and Clubs, and out of town villages. I was enjoying myself. Alright, alright, being a fan with a brain and supposedly more money, and not quite one of them. But even in spite of being put on a superior and aloof and suspicious pedestal I didn't want, it was alright.

The band—it was an ordinary, better than most rock 'n' roll bands. It played because it liked playing, and because it brought in a bit of pin money. But the kid from the posh end, the singer, now he had ambition. Like Cliff Richard he wanted to make the vocal grade at the top, the Big Time. He loved the music and he was with it all along and possibly more than any of the others, but he had this ambition and no idea of how to do it, of how to get on. He'd ask me.

One of the things this group needs is publicity. See we only get the crumbs, what the Clubs can't fill in any other way. We could do with our own club in Leicester, like that '2 I's'* place down in London.

---

* Coffee bar in Old Compton Street, London. Birthplace of British skiffle music.

You want publicity?

Why, could you do anything?

Might get the local papers to do a feature, but it'd need a line. Something to tag the story on to.

Oh.

Well, what about — the band that can't get the bookings? The Clubs aren't the greatest. They don't really like our kind of music. What we need is a club of our own for the teenagers who like our kind of music.

And so the press turned up — *Beat Group can't get a look in* — and I wasn't even there. I had done the work to get the press to turn up. I was pleased. It had worked. It was the first time I'd ever done anything like that. I'd enjoyed it. The lads liked it.

But what about this show of our own, this place of our own idea. It had been brooded on, and was coming out in the open.

We'd need a hall.

I tell you what, you find the hall, take the can, look after the money side and the organisation and all that and we'll put on the show. If you make anything it's yours. After all you're the one with the brain to run the thing.

Alright, fair enough. The idea had formed. A club, a show, a dance run for young people by young people. Us getting together to run our own show for us.

By this time I'd left University. I planned to make a short trip, try to raise enough money to put on a few shows for August and September. Money was the problem. The group hadn't got it, and they looked to me, the man with the brain to find it, to have it. It was understood that if there was any profit it would be mine. I would have the rake-off. And if there was a loss, then I made it up. I was to carry the can. They would operate the shows. It was my gamble, my idea. I had the vested interest. I came back from my tour with enough money to book on two shows, and I booked a central hall for two nights, consecutive Friday nights at the end of August. I hadn't any money for more than this. See how two went and then think again, and there was the mistake, one of the great technical mistakes. I should have found enough money to float a whole series, possibly ten to twenty to see properly whether the idea would work financially or not, to give it a real and fair trial.

The two shows came off, and the money more than ran out. The first show cost £24 to put on, including the hire of the hall and the pay-out to the bands, adverts in the press and so on. Around 75 people turned up at 2/6 a time, and possibly more than 25 without paying. With refreshments the total take in was around £12. This made a loss of £11. But it was thought a great success, an omen for a fabulous future. The only dance in town run by the lads for the lads — *Chez Ray Rock*.

The second on the following Friday cost to put on just over £20. Around 150 people turned up at 2/6 a time, and around 50 got in free. With refreshments we took in just under £20. The band again were paid, and we broke even all bar a couple of bob. It was an even greater success. But it was the end. The next week the hall had been booked by someone else. I was in debt. I hadn't any more cash. It was all over. Altogether, including my own direct expenses which hadn't been included in the cost of the shows, I finished up some £50 in debt. I couldn't afford another show. No one else could. The thing was over. Finished.

Why did the band have to be paid? It was a joint programme. I had found the capital. They had arranged the show. Why pay the band? It's a stupid question to ask. To run the show the band had to provide their own guitars, record player, microphone, amplifier, and all these things cost money, either to hire or to buy on the HP. There could be over £200 of kit on that stage. It all has to be paid for. They had done that. To play at their own dance, they had to give up what could, would or was in fact a commercial booking. I paid the lowest I could. They accepted the lowest they dare. It meant a big drop playing at the dance. This no one minded, but they simply couldn't have managed if they were to be expected to play for nothing or, worse, expected to finance the business side. To move their equipment from where it was stored to the hall for the dance cost money, and no expenses were paid out, from a suburb to the hall and back the taxi fare could easily come to over 15/–. It was impossible and unfair to expect or even to hope they'd come in with their own money, to subsidise the hire of the hall, the capital stuff.

But there were other things we lacked, that could so easily— if only I'd thought—have been avoided, and so we could have kept going. Again with money. If instead of borrowing a few pounds, I'd borrowed a couple of hundred there'd have been a chance. But there was no faith. I had no faith. I had to find my own feet. This was the way I was doing it. Oh, I know now I could so easily have borrowed a couple of hundred, pushing my luck and using my charms. But no, no faith, no guts. It's easy looking back but...

Lend us a couple of quid. I want to run this dance. Only need a couple of quid—and if only there'd been faith; if only rather than scrat around friends, I'd gone straight to the point, not to someone I knew would lend me a few pounds in any case, but to someone who'd got a real few bob, and might if I convinced him.

Look, I haven't a penny, but I've got an idea. I think it'll work, very hopeful, great chances. It runs like this ... But I need a couple of hundred. You might never see it again, but you know me. I'll pay it back to you, tanner a week. You'll get it back in the end.

Second was a complete lack of any long-term planning. Again I wasn't convinced, and I hadn't really tried to convince anybody else that the idea was fabulous and it stood a good chance. And so we only ran for two nights. And then when we wanted to book up again, we couldn't. They wouldn't, couldn't fit us in. The dates had been booked. But when the first of the Fridays were booked there was an empty book, an empty space on every Friday for weeks ahead. Once again, an imagination, a conviction would have got us through. How about it? Every Friday from now through ninety weeks. There's a booking for you. Pay you now, cash for the first ten, and deposit for the rest. There's something for you. But no. No faith.

And third. I was on my own. Again, half convinced I hadn't believed to the point where I could convince others to come in with me on the capital side, not just money, but the background work that could have made it a success. I was on my own. I was business manager, originator, ideas man, stage manager, ticket puncher, money taker, bouncer, financial backer; the whole shoot rolled into one. If there had been just two more people, in the background, two civil servants, two workers. Ah, but perhaps because there was no control was why it worked so well? No, no. It worked in spite of this chaos, not because of it. There was a romance about it, a glamour; but that could have been kept, and enhanced with a little organisation. The chaos that there was, it was bad. I'd have to pick on some kid I'd never seen before in my life and say — look here, can you look after the cash and don't let anyone in without paying till I get back. I say, can you sort that crowd out by the door, looks like a spot of trouble there. I had to do almost the whole bloody thing myself. And I was the only responsible person in the eyes of the people who had so kindly consented to my hire of their hall. The guitarist coming through to the front door where I was selling tickets, the caretaker's going to close the hall and call the police. There's a lad out there and he's brought a bottle of beer in with him. The caretaker says we can't use the microphone any more and we've had to 'cause ours got broke, and so you'd better see the caretaker. Look, this isn't very good, is it? I don't mind you having a good time, but drinking, well it just won't do. Look, they never told me anything about you being able to use the microphone, and one of your young men has been sitting on the grand piano, and my guv'nor gave me strict instructions to close the building if anyone sat on the grand piano. The Women's Labour gave us that last year, and it cost a lot of money. And in the background there'd be noises, very audible — tell the snivel-nosed bastard if he don't shut his cake hole, we'll play noughts and crosses with his bleeding poker face. Go tell him get nutted, our Ray. It's alright; they don't mean it. Shut up will you. Drive you daft. You'd run down to the front door and — look darling, if you want to get stuffed that bad do you mind using the waste ground at the back of the hall, luv, there's a good girl, and pull yourself together before you move off — and past the kid you left holding the cash, him saying — look here, mate, I'm not going to sit here looking after your money all night — and across the road and into the pub, just to get away for three quick minutes. Ah, it's him, he's the man in charge, better ask him. Look, my mate's a singer, he's alright is my mate. Can't you fix him up so he gets a song in 'cause the band up there don't like him 'cause he won the Palais miming contest off them last week. Alright, alright, I'll see. Can I have my money now please, Chez. I got to go on nightshift. Come on will you. I got to fire a train all the way down to Cricklewood at ten. Alright, alright, shut up. Look, I can't look after your money any more, and there's two big chaps said they wouldn't pay. You better see them 'cause it isn't fair them getting in for nowt while I paid and got stuck sitting in this doorway taking the money off everybody, now is it, it isn't fair. No, no, alright, alright; give us half a chance.

And at the end of the night some kid handed me twenty-odd pounds; and someone thanked me for letting them have a sing, and the kid from the posh end, the key vocalist came up protesting that he'd been used, and all the programme he'd worked out had been knocked out because I wanted to let some dirty old Ted in a bloody drape suit have a sing. Look, he aint a Ted, and it aint a drape suit, and he can sing, and he's got the feel of the thing, and that's what this whole show thing is for. Well, if that's all, you can count me out on any more, because all the time I put into working out a programme and you come along and mess it all up. And the caretaker — I found sixteen beer bottles under the seats around the sides.

Did you indeed? (Nice bit of pin money for you, on the empties.) Yes, and there's no need to be funny, and I bet not one of them kids were over eighteen. Liar. Well, and what about the bloody grand piano? You and your bloody grand piano.

No, it had worked. But with just one other person in the background, just one other to help carry the can it could have gone on; with just a little more faith and guts it could have gone on; a little more organisation, a little more planning. I went back to the flat after a meal with those left, and when I thought over what happened; how it had worked and got so near — it nearly broke me.

There was only one thing to do — get out of town, and do the grand tour all over again. Find enough money to clear off the last show, and enough to start working on a third. And so I went. I came back after about a month in October, and took a flat on the Ditch Road. It was a wonderful flat. It was just off central, and private, less neighbours, no *concièrge*, no landlord you ever saw; only the estate agent who called for the rent. It was over a Ladies Hairdressing, with all the smell, but there was constant hot water, day and night and a bath. From my one room I could see and count thirteen factory chimneys, thirteen of them. I took a job back on the railways-shifts, wonderful peculiar shifts, with the chance of much overtime. I could earn up to, and sometimes over, £15 a week. It was a hard time, but if I worked it right I could traipse up to the University, and round the Town and write letters and all that, and fit it all in. I got put on the phone. It was a cold winter. I never had enough blankets on the bed to keep me warm. It was cold that winter. The phone did for an alarm clock.

Getting up at four in the morning, and down to the station and working through in the open air to four in the afternoon, and then back to the flat, working on my own for one, two hours, out in the Town by about six and back before eleven. Sleep, and then up again at four. It was all worth it. Apart from being hungry and cold, it was alright; and in any case it was better than being back at that University, full-time. Things started to move.

I was not only getting the feel of the Town, but getting to know the people on the Town, and beginning to use the beaten tracks. Tuesdays down at the Palais — 2/6 disc night. On these Tuesday night sessions there was a short talent contest. It was here that our vocalist, the kid with the guitar from the posh end, got beaten in the voting by a local team of three. The Three sang in a straight vocal way rather like Gene Vincent, singing for the laughs and the immediate impact. This Three had sung a couple of numbers at our own shows, but it was when they were on at the Palais in competition with our own vocalist that the difference came out and it was a clear cut difference, a difference much greater than a mere difference in style or type of song.

The kid from the posh end put his number across à la Cliff Richard, in a soft style. It was beat taken more from the stories of success, taken from wanting to be a Pop Singer; tied up with the Man and the Hope and the '2I's'. Whereas the other group, the Three, had their roots in the Town, for the lads; in the same tradition as the skiffle of the early days in Soho playing to a known, sympathetic audience, as Country and Western, as jazz of the jazz clubs rather than the jazz of the Flamingo; from the same traditions as the pub and piano bars of the back streets. With the Three there was contact between the audience and the singer, an intimacy of the sort that you get in cabaret, really good shows put on particularly in working men's clubs in the North. It was — get up our kid will you — and our kid gets up and gives a song, rather than the other — the posh ender for whom it was — I like beat and that kind of music and the idea of beat as I've seen it on television and I think I could sing like that, and be a Pop Singer. Now this and the way it comes across is more or less what I like to call the soft thing. And for it to get across it needs a tremendous build up, and has to rely on the technical brilliance of the backing groups. It's very much more difficult to get across in the flesh than in a recording studio. It's essentially synthetic. And it doesn't take at all well to the closed circuit, to the immediacy and intimacy of the clubs, or the upper room at a pub. With the other there was this intimacy, this contact, and also musically it went back much further through Gene Vincent to Johnny Cash, Country and Western and had assimilated these into something very immediate with an impact that came across to a particular group of listeners, participants almost, in Leicester. Often now, when I hear certain records I keep wishing they did the little Leicester bits I got used to while I was there; the way of saying certain words, certain inflections, a certain way of getting a number across that was peculiar to Leicester, and wonderful and fabulous and very original and new. It was this I liked, and it was this I was after — the sense of contact and getting across to the people rather than some starry-eyed kid, however good, singing to the roof like to the angel of the Lord, or this big Man with the fat cigar who was going to hear

and take him up into Cadillac Land. No, it was the intimacy
that appealed to me, this was what I liked, the sense of
exclusion, a closed circuit and yet in an open room, rather like
the drinking clubs (some only) in Soho, the show night at a
big CIU* club, the upper room at a pub; the sense of contact
that comes over in a floor show, a local talent contest, a local
jazz club; something that's warm and close and immediate.

From a handout that never went out — November 1959.

WHAT WE OFFER YOU

```
Well, we can't offer the plush and the chic
of the Palais, or Il Rondo, or the Adelphi.
We cannot offer you that. At the moment we
haven't even a permanent home. We haven't got
the money. We are not going to give you the
records of London or Americi. What we can do,
what we do want to offer you is your own
show. The people who run it, those who sing
and the boys of the band are all living in
Leicester. You, the people in Leicester are
being offered the best that you yourselves can
do. As often as we can we will run a Club and
a Dance like the Oh Boy Session we ran at the
Co-op Hall. If you think you can sing, or
strum a guitar, or play a piano, or do any-
thing like that, you've only to let us know,
come to one of the two practices we hold in
the week, and if you really can do something,
then you can go on the next Club or Dance.
And when will the next be? Today we haven't a
clue, but if we know tomorrow, and we might,
then you'll know too. If you really want
another one, then there will be another one,
```

---

* Club and Institute Union.

you can be sure of that, and don't worry,
we'll let you know as soon as we know ourselves. It's your own show we're asking you to
support. It's your own people we're asking you
to dance to, and to dance with, or just to
listen and watch. The more of you who come;
the more of you who perform, the bigger all
this will become. If it flops, it will be
your fault. If it becomes even hotter than the
posh places, then it will be because of you.
All we can offer you then, is your own image.
If you think that image is good, if you think
Leicester the city without the theatre can do
as well as anywhere else, then join in with
us. We don't care what you wear, but we do
care whether you support your own people or
not. We think you should. We are not going to
give you nylons and nighties as prizes. We are
going to give you whatever we find of the
best in the city. If you have any comments,
any ideas, bright or otherwise, then let us
know. So that is what we offer you yourselves,
your own city, and we hope, and we think,
that you'll enjoy yourselves, that you'll join
in, and make your own ball, because, boys and
girls, it's all yours.

Now, the appeal in that was for something inclusive, everyone
welcome. This is an important thing: exclusive or inclusive.
What was at the back of my own mind?

A place like The Chequers on Friday nights. The
Chequers was a large central pub, a big boozer with a juke
box downstairs, and on Friday nights they let the top room
where a band which included the Three played from eight to
half ten, or ten. It was very alive, tough and fast. In theory the
top room was an open part of the pub, anyone could go up.
But in fact it was restricted principally to those out for a night

on the Town. It was the pub for Friday nights. It was the pub that put on the Lads' own band, and the band played numbers at the request of the lads and allowed the lads their own chance to get up and sing. It was closed, in fact, shut up in the old traditions of the big boozer band night, almost strictly under 25 age group. It was good. The music was nearly always good. And the atmosphere was tremendous, and it was in theory open — no club cards, no restrictions imposed by the management. But it was closed in that being all there was. The band played for the money the landlord paid them. The landlord got a large take-in on increased sales. The lads had a night out, and a chance to listen and participate with their own band. There was nothing else. There was little room for experiment. For two hours it was fabulous and fantastic and after that there was nothing.

What I had at the back of my own mind was something like this that didn't finish after two hours, but went on, and something that wasn't strictly commercial but where there was a background administration. What sort of administration? Dave put it better than I could once, when he said what we were after was a central agency, an umbrella organisation which could run two-hour booze and band sessions, large dances, coffee bar, boxing, football, a whole range of social services and amusements and entertainments, including being there to help anyone who wanted any help, from financial trouble to any personal problems, with advice or information.

What we had to look for in November was a place where we could start the dances up again and hold the ideas that had gathered around us who were running the old dances, and around me, that could hold all this together. I very nearly got just the thing—a basement in a central street, all day, all night, low rental, no trouble, almost ideal—but it fell through. I was back on looking for halls for hire for one night or two, short series.

I couldn't get, and hadn't, the money for the big hall we had used before, but we got a small hall at the back of the police station. It was an impossible place in an impossible location, but it had to do. The floor was like Brighton beach. The lighting was like one of these new Income Tax offices. The stage was like any church hall, and of course it was right at the back of the police station. We dare not charge any more than 1/6. On the first dance 20 people paid to come in. We made a loss of about £2. But there were over 20 people in the bands, with vocalists, hangers-on, and helpers. It was all worthwhile, even if only in that it held the hard core of operators together. The dances ran through to the end of the year with never more than 50 people paying. Always they made a loss. The loss was made up by me with my doing overtime on the railway. I'd work a Sunday night and do as much overtime as I could to keep the thing going. The bands worked for expenses only, sometimes less than that. But it still needed all the bravado I could muster to keep the debtors away. But it was in the right direction. Only the hall was wrong. And the constant lack of money, and there was nothing we could do about this. But it was in the right direction.

. . .

From the Leicester press:

Rock 'n' roll *à la carte*. That's how you might describe a
new venture by some lively teenagers… As the handbill
says "run by the boys for the boys". But we might also
add "girls" because if you want to jive you need a
partner… They do their own arranging of popular
songs, helped by Bill Prendegast, who, in the words of
"Eugene", "has the knack of picking out the right songs.

It was alright, if only, but only money. Desperate. Must have
money. I was keeping up and making new friends up at the
University, and there was a growing idea that there might be
a way of getting money from public funds. It could, this thing
we were doing, come under the 'youth work' sections. It was
an idea. It smelt a little. But it was an idea. In fact it seemed
the only way.

And there were nights round at my pad and afternoons at
Jimmy's palace. The night the lads, all fifteen of them, turned
up at my place and we tried getting a kip down for a couple
of hours, and then getting up ever so early Sunday morning,
fair kill you, and the old couple from upstairs coming down
into the bathroom and finding about ten of the lads in it,
cleaning shoes, washing, and everyone creating; and then out
in the morning round to a caff and playing on the machines
for a couple of hours. Assing about with this skull I'd gotten
hold of, a thing we called Oscar — Oscar, where are you,
Oscar. Walking round the room with this skull. I kept away
from work through the last part of December and most of
January, and in these two months of freedom the pace really
worked itself out, into something so fast, so high-powered. It
was an omen for the future. There were the laughs and the

arguments and the dreams and I was in. I wasn't sitting in the background any more. I was in the thick of it.

A letter to — I'm not sure quite who. It was one of the letters that got passed around a great deal, and one of the very few I've salvaged.

Dear Sir,

I last wrote to you about ten days ago, and in case you didn't receive my letter, have forgotten it, or considered it of no importance I am writing again. On Thursday, between 7 and 11 in the evening, behind the police station in Charles Street, at St. George's Hall, there is a dance, and I should welcome you. Every night in every part of the city there are dances. Why should this one be so special? There will not be hundreds of people. It is not in aid of anything. No one of any importance will be there. A few records will be played, and a few tin pot skiffle groups will make a deafening noise through electrical devices, and a few grubby lads and louts will bellow words into a microphone. You wouldn't know what they said if you hadn't heard them so many times before. On a grubby floor a few kids with strong Leicester accents will do their best to dance the way they do on the telly, and will painfully fail. A fat young man in a greasy duffle coat will stand at the door and take two shillings from any of the city's youth who brave the weather to come to such a drab and cold hall. And so what's so special? Had an idea: thought you might like to come.

A lot of people spend a lot of time talking about, writing about, thinking about, doing something about lads and lassies who come from what they call the 'working class' districts of cities and towns. *Great thoughts have emerged, works of art have arisen, imaginations and intellects have been stirred, and some good work has been done; but much of the work that has been done, to help, has been out of contact with the mood of the people it's trying to help. The youth club, group, venture, organisations, of the Co-ops, the Boys' Clubs, the Labour Party, University Missions, Chapels, Churches, Civic organisations, are often it is to be regretted out of contact; and so many of the high ideals, bright ideas of all these helpers do not connect with their subjects.*

What does connect? What is in contact? — Oh, the heart-shaped bar at the Palais where one can sip coca cola, iced, through a straw and listen to a glam girl spinning the latest on disc every lunch hour. The Mecca organisation makes a nice profit. On Monday a Mecca share stood at 31/9 — not bad. There's nothing wrong in that. They're in business to make money, and they do a good job — keeping the kids off the streets. This is all very noble. There are a large number of people making a large amount of money, and at the same time doing this wonderful job of keeping the kids off the streets — no one could wish for anything better.

I do. At the moment it's just a tin-pot dance, and it doesn't even break even. But it keeps them off the streets — like the Palais, only it's colder. It gives them something to do — like the Palais, they can make a noise into a micro-phone, only there's less to hear it.

And so what is so special?

Nothing but an idea — to bridge that gap between those with the high ideals, and good intentions, those who care and do not make contact; and the commercials who make contact but don't care.

It won't work.

It doesn't work. There isn't any money — haven't even enough for the adverts this week. But no one knows about it. If they did there might be some money, Having made a something out of a large loss in the past, it is possible that with a little money in the future one could go a long way. And then get a proper permanent hall, just for the boys, a club, and then there might be something of value.

Here in Leicester there is a University — over 1,000 students, some of whom, a very few, care, are concerned, and are involved with what for want of a better name one can call "Le Peuple".

Nearly a century ago similar people from similar institutions went out into the working-class wilds of South London and did a great deal of good. The "Old Left" that helped to inspire them is dying, but a New Left is taking its place, and inspiring others, only they don't go out into the wilds any more, many of them come from the wilds; and from them may come something of value.

I want once again to invite you to come. It's just a tiddly little dance run by a few arty farties. It won't be no cop at all chip. But that's not the point.

It's the idea behind it all, and from it there might come, in time, something of value.

Yours,

RAY GOSLING.

And then we were in. Everything happened. We were in the youth business. Everything except money. And so they came from London. I met them. The lads, who by this time had become a committee, met them. The University, who by this time had become a Trustee body, met them. We were in, in this youth business. I didn't like it.

No, they hadn't got it. The whole teenage thing, the whole of the thing that started the dances and the shows and had got these people together — the idea is running a business, and not a club. Look, don't youth clubs, all the ones I know, work like that? The Them running the business, and the members running the club. Where's the revolution in this? And most of the lads were very polite and said as has been said for bleeding centuries — yes, yes, yes, this is what we want — yes, yes, yes, you are so right — and then when the Money, the Them had left, they turned on me, to a man every one of this committee turned on me.

You were rude, bad mannered. You never thought of us.

Look, they've got the money, use your nut will you, Ray.

Not on them conditions. They'd run the show. They'd take over. We wouldn't have a say. I wouldn't. You wouldn't. Bloody London would run it.

And then from the others, the ones who'd been in it from the start when it was trying to build up a singer, and a band and a set of dances. What's the future in it for us? All that talk about records and the people he knows, and all that show business stuff. Did he ever see how we played? Did he ever make any offers for us? Did he ever say anything about a record for us, bookings for our bands? Do you think we've helped you, Ray, just to see a youth club. No?

But there's something in what that man said. They've got the money. You've got to listen to them, Ray.

Rot, I tell you rot. They haven't got that much; and in any case they want to chew your balls off and put you all out in fancy dress and all twee twee. Leave you with nothing you can call your own. They'll drag you into their system, and their system it's always the same — they run the thing, not you, however much they may kid you on that you do run it, you won't. It won't be yours.

Look, what you got agin him, eh? Did you ask him for a job, and he turn you down? We notice you spent a lot of time with him. Bet you didn't talk about this all the time. What have you got against him?

I told you. They're no good. It's the same as before only all dressed up.

Shut up. Now listen, Ray, you're going to see them tomorrow again, right. Well, he said it all depends. Well, give it a fair try will you? It's us as well as you, you know.

Alright then, just as you say — a fair try.

Tell us, why won't you let us come along too? Why do you always have to do all this bargaining yourself?

I tell you. Because if you went along with me, every time they'd twist as they do, and you'd say as you've said tonight, yes, yes, you're alright, that's what we want — and they'll promise you things, always things — like a juke box, a coffee bar, a dance hall — always things. And as long as they do that, and as long as you say that's what you want and that you want no more things, they'll always be the same — they'll run the show. The whole idea is that you, us, we should control this thing, operate it ourselves and for ourselves.

And then as always my little speech. I want to get out from Leicester, as soon as I can. But when I go it's got to be one of you that moves into my place.

We needed the money, strings or no strings. It was strings. The press did us well *Leicester's New Youth Club — twelve men and a girl to run the show*, the committee, a photo of each man and they were the supreme body, the executive, the ruling clique of a scheme, an idea that we saw as a big thing, a whole organisation run by us for us, with coffee bar, dance halls. Anything we wanted, we needed, that place was going to give us — and give us as our right — our own place.

The difference between Us and Them was very slender. It was a difference of emphasis, not fact. They wanted to see in operation very much the same sort of things as we did. But for us, it was to be Us running it, having control, complete control. For Them, the young people were to look after the activities, beneath their umbrella organisation. It's a very slender difference, but it makes all the activity, all the organisation have a completely alien slant. It isn't ours, unless we actually physically control it, Then, it's ours.

. . .

This happened through January, February and in March. I became the full-time secretary to the committee. The first job was to find a temporary site, a large central building we could use until our own permanent one could be built. In fact the committee was holding the power and taking the decisions. We were in fact running the show, though in the background even then were the Monies, the Them.

We'd found these temporary premises from the City Council, and we'd looked them over and they'd do, and we'd worked out how much money we'd need, and what would fit in where, which wall would have to come down. And the fire people looked round, and the others, and it went back to the City Council. The Council had doubts. I tried to convince them. Alright, they'd look it over personally with me. I went back to our own committee. We've got it. It's in the bag. I went over the building with the City Council. They asked me to wait in the road outside. The Chairman came out. No. We are sorry, but now we have seen it personally we have to say No. I have to go back to tell my own committee this, and it will be a blow to them. I'm going to be out of a job, the idea is going to fold up if I have to tell them now that we've had it, now after I've promised this temporary building. Look, can you find us another and quick.

Alright, we the City Council will do our best. Trust in us.

Fair enough. I see you tomorrow.

I went back to my committee — liar — no confidence — get out.

Let me have one more try.

Look, we gave up the dances. Thought there'd be this new building. Takes time you say. Let's look for a temporary site. Find one. You say you've found one. That's what you said. It's in the bag. And now it isn't. Turns out you're a liar. We just can't trust you anymore.

Give me a week. Give me a week. One week.

Right. One week, and no site and then you're out. Out for good. Back to the City Council. I got a week. Find us, please. The Council were wonderful. They turned up again, both places were right in the centre. We had to be in the centre of the town. We looked this new place over, good, central; but stack full of hosiery machinery. How can you get the machinery out? We don't know. It isn't ours. Whose is it? Don't know, we better find out. But can we have it when we get the machinery out? It'll have to go to Council, and then there's the fire people. Can I take a chance and make another promise to our committee? That's your worry, but I think you'll be alright.

Right. Back to our committee. Don't worry.

What you mean?

It's in the bag, almost.

And in comes London. What's happening? Wasting your time. Getting paid from our funds and doing nothing. Not good enough. We want action, not words.

Shut up, get lost. If you don't want me, I'll go. Shut up talking. You're getting on me from all sides, and I'm doing all I can.

Find out facts. We want action. No airy fairy ideas and half promises this time.

Right — and back to the City Council. Yes — but — forget the buts — right — yes — on a piece of paper. Put it in the post for you. Fair enough. Open the post.

A letter, all bleeding buts. Showed the letter — not good enough. Right, back, again, to Council.

We need the fire people to see it. See the fire people, personally. Make it now — alright — yes, but. Forget the buts. We can't, we're the fire people. Bugger the fire people. The police, alright, alright, tomorrow.

And back to the Lads, to the committee I worked for.

Look, do you trust me?

No.

Look, will you give me a vote of confidence; or let me clear off? Come on, if you want me I'll stay. If you don't I'll go. — We have to trust you, don't we. There's nobody else. We got no choice. That's the nearest you'll get to your vote of confidence.

Alright. Thank you.

Ah, come on Ray, come on, buy us a drink; come out on Town alright — Trust in the Council.

It worked. We did trust in the Council, and we were glad that we did trust in the Council, for they were, considering, very very good.

And we were the bosses, every one a little boss. When the staff got appointed, it was us. We cleaned the building, painted it, staffed it, and we were going to run it. And all the while, was Money. It was open, on the town, a caff and centre run by us, for us. It was beginning to work.

But this was September, October, November. It started as the caff run by the lads, for the lads; grass roots, ground level.

Manchester Guardian, Nov. 7th
A youth club experiment — attracting the rough and roaring.
Attracting the rough and roaring as if what we wanted to do was to draw into the civilised youth club world all these roaring unclubbables; as if we were in some superior position with some new quality that gave us the chance to attract unclubbables into a club, and turn them out finished products for the ... tell me the old, old story. That's the way the idea had gone. All I had to do, was to find a way out. Quietly, decently, without any fuss I should go. Or fight, fight till they asked me to resign.

No, what we set out to do was to make a world outside the established set-up look after itself, and keep itself alive; not a social service to a people; but a centre for a community, the centre being actually and completely controlled by that community.

.   .   .

They, the backers, wanted to see us as a club drawing unclubbables into a youth club, and so into the better life; as a new and exciting venture giving the chance to those who hadn't so far been given this chance of moving upwards; not outwards or inwards or across, but up. And the parents of the people who came to the club, they too for the most part saw it this way, as something that was keeping people off the streets, keeping their own sons and daughters out of mischief, and giving their children another of the chances they never had. And the kids, the patrons, the members themselves; for them too it was a road upwards. It was fun and a laugh and it was looked on as being alright by the authorities.

While for just a few of us it was something that could, that stood a chance of breaking right across a whole tradition, a tradition that stifled both the teenage business and the authority's youth service. A moving across, an opening out without a moving into the nice dead world that was the aim for both the traditional youth clubs and the commercial organisations.

This couldn't be done. It was inevitable, in the situation itself, irrespective of the personalities involved, of the city or the way the press began to treat us.

But on we went, and on I went. Hanging on to the little we had.

The committees thinking they owned the place, and rightly so. The staff who had to run the place, in spite of and because of the committee. The friends of the staff and the friends of the committee who thought they had a right to be in on everything. Committee meeting after committee meeting. And the thing went on. The trouble, the real trouble was that we took the thing so bloody seriously. We were really worried over the pilfering. We were really worried lest the whole thing should fall apart. We were too young for things to be taken in their stride. Slowly the old committee began to break up and this worried us, but really it was inevitable. They had built the thing up, given night after night to get the thing going, and now it was going there were so many things they had to catch up on.

I took a holiday, seven days on the coast away from it all. The pace and the worry of the thing was extreme. All the time it was like you were sitting on a bomb waiting for it to go off. You were in the thick of things and couldn't get out. I went back on the Saturday night, very late and there were two broken chairs, a broken table, blood all over the floor, and seven pounds gone from the till. Worried, something had to be done. Call in the police. Daft sods we were. What was seven pounds, two broken chairs and a broken table? What was it really? Oh, but there was London,* all the while after facts, figures — why no great profit, why such great bills, such big wage pay outs? Why no formal club, why no paid-up

---

* The charitable foundation funding the club was administered from the captial.

members, why no activities? The pressure began to get put on. Security got tightened up, a little. The committee eventually agreed to membership, for the back half of the building only. But the thing was beginning to stink — membership, the idea of going all formal and looking for activities. We ran dances upstairs. Why the loss? Bands have to be paid — why pay bands? They should do it for nothing. The room wasn't big enough for dances. But the thing still worked.

The slow disintegration began to set in, and all the time I kept working ways of keeping the two together — the old idea and Money. The crumble began of the staff; in the absolute power of the committee; in my own power; the power of the staff, and the power of the ground level committee and ruling clique that set the thing up. The slow weeding out of patrons over twenty, the hard cores; of the open society and open doors policy; and it moved into a strict membership for young people, youths, children; the real kiddoes moving in.

And with all this the internal troubles — the fights. And then came trouble, real trouble. It was an afternoon just before Christmas. There was a crowd upstairs, drunk and a fight and a wreckage; and we'd got nobody strong enough to tackle it, and the general public outside in the street were phoning for the police, and the police came and four got arrested and we had become witnesses for the prosecution. Oh, it was bound to come sooner or later, we'd have to show that we were not so free and easy that we could put up with everything. But the thing came as a shock. People had always looked on us as being not just a sort of home, but somewhere where things were so free and easy that although you may have only come in for a coffee, in fact you really ran the place, or had the right to. I had to sign a statement over the damage, and at the Magistrates it was read out. I had called the cops. I had turned agin the lads. My flat got broken into. Threats, all that. The lads were kept in custody over Christmas. We closed the place up one morning when it looked really bad, and I went south for Christmas, out of the town.

The night before it took place we were talking, us and the same people who we had to sign the statement a few days later, talking of new ideas, of an extension, an upper room turned into something a little more exclusive, for an older crowd. Sad not just because the next day the cops had to be called in on the same few, but sad because all the ideas coming out they didn't mean a thing. The crumble was well under way. I came back from London and there were meetings, and new promises of support; and any trouble again call us in, will you. And none of it meant a thing. It was over. The crumble was the only thing that kept sweeping on, relentlessly.

And then the pamphlet, and the press—*Mirror*, *Chronicle*, *Sketch*; and then the locals—pressmen I knew. Pressmen who knew what I was getting at. Old Bob, we sat in the pub we'd sat in before when the old crowd was on the paper.

Look, Ray, I've got to do a story tonight.

Yes. You know the way I meant that pamphlet.

I do, but the nationals have had their dabble and I've got to do the bit for us; and after all you did write it. I mean it can't be a lie.

No, look, I tell you something. A man stops me in the street the other day, one of our city fathers and he says—we're going to get you out of this town if it's the last thing we do. Go on, jump on the thing with your two flat-footed moral boots, jump on it with them. It'll be a wonderful story.

And back at the club — I'll kill you — what you say that for — why, why, why did you have to say that? Look, I know it's the truth, but why did you have to say it?

And then Georgie Pollock from *Reynolds** came down, and he spent three days on the town, and tried to find out and he was the only pressman who did and he said it's alright. I think you'll weather the storm, and the idea will too. Jim thought we would. The loyal few thought we would. But no, the crumble had gone too far, much too far. I was on the road out. January, February, stop.

Coming into Leicester on the Nottingham diesel.

I want you to resign.

Why?

Three reasons.

The ancient three. I know them. I can tell you. The standard reasons for a diplomatic departure. They never fail. There's always that little bit of truth in them. I am tired, very tired.

You listen to me. First, let's face it, you have done nothing. You haven't organised the activities we expected you would.

You are right. I don't believe in activities, not like that. Guilty on that one.

Secondly, you haven't been straight on money.

Right again. Guilty, but let me say this. I have lived in this thing, and worked with it and for it in that city for nearly two years. I have enjoyed it. I have loved it, and I have done all I

---

* *Reynolds News*, Sunday newspaper run by the Co-Operative Party.

could, and when I leave that city I shall have to square my debts over £500, and you know why — yes Shirley's got a suit, Dog's got a sweater, Dave I could tell you, and on and on. I've been soft. I'm soft by nature. I shall be sorry to go. I like that city, so much.

Don't rant on, please listen, on the third count...

Whether on that I am guilty or not guilty it doesn't matter. I just don't want it mentioned. If anyone touches on that... No leave that alone. You don't meddle there. I shall go. I shall do as you say.

And back at the club for the last week. Walking up the stairs to the office.

I've waited a long time. You sent them down. You went over to the law. They do time because of you. You deserve this.

Right. Maybe I do.

From the lads a beating because I was supposed to have gone over to the law. From the Bosses a beating because I was too much one of the lads, I wouldn't play right and decent.

It's not true, neither of those. I hadn't gone over to the law. I was never one of the lads. Me, being me, both those were impossible, laughable if they hadn't been believed.

I spent the night in hospital. I went over Nottingham to give a lecture with this great big black eye, knowing that it was all over; and when I got back to the flat there was a crowd of lads waiting for me — a farewell party, one last big ball before I went. And people said that it was all over, the idea was finished. No, when the witch-hunt has died down and people no longer see me around the streets, when things quieten down there's a chance again. And the promises came in — we're with you, Ray — the one thing that kept me going, that had stopped me from leaving before I had to.

Forget it. It'll pass over. We were just mad at you. You done a lot of daft things. And Moosh sitting in the office at the club just like it was all starting over again, people making plans, new committees, new ideas just like it was going to go on, just the same, just like before.

And then a Sunday afternoon, and the light shone through the window and no one said very much, and the light through the window. I couldn't see anybody's face, kept smoking, black eye kept aching; and Hoggart said: We'll fight on, if you want us to. You know that.

It were like the lads the night before, looking round at these faces only just seeing blurs out of one eye, and the light kept coming through this window. No, they stood by me; Norman and Joan and Richard, and Dog and Moosh and Jimmy and Cadman.

No. No more fight. The end of the road. I handed over my set of keys, and they drove me round to the club. One man left now, out of the old crowd, only one man. It's up to you now, our Jim, it's up to you.

Never said no more farewells but that one. I went out. Up the street and coming down just like it was old times was the same crowd that made the witch-hunt and gave me the black eye, and we shook hands.

You're alright, Ray. It's just that you're a bit daft at times, like most of us.

It was all over. They'd got the chance, make me into a black angel and paint themselves white, and get away with it, and they stood a chance.

For me, it was back on the roam everywhere I could round and round in circles from north to south to east to west working off all the months I'd spent in that city, working it all right out of my system; and then joining the queue at the Labour Exchange, it was like a penance back at Northampton and taking a job, any job, just a job—please. It was over, all over, bar a great big lump of debt.

.   .   .

Why did it fail?

It didn't fail. It didn't fail. The trials and the fights and the articles and the pamphlet and the lectures and the talk and the thefts and the staff troubles—they were nothing; nothing compared with the greatness and the laughs and the sense of the place being a home. And then Dave left. And then I left. And then Jim left. And it was over. And it was over because the ones with the money, the backers; they wouldn't take the step of faith—the step that would have given them a chance to look at the laughs from that place. No, we were supposed to be in business for the good of the people; but slowly it dawned on them that neither I nor any of the staff were in the business for the good of others, however much we kidded ourselves. We were in it for the love and laughs, for the love of the people, and the love of our jobs, and the wonderful feeling of doing something we wanted to do for ourselves and our own, and the laughs and happiness other people got from it.

But it wasn't just the backers. It was that the people who used the place, they couldn't for the most part grasp what was happening, and that applied to me. Centuries of being told what to do, unless you've got the money and can tell others what to do; and then right in front of your eyes, you got no one telling you what to do. You got all the freedom and all the power and you don't know what to do. You want to get back to that factory, where you knew where you stood. You see we were in a class on our own, only we never really knew it. We were all of one class, the privileged class; and all we could do was what we'd been trained to do, gripe and moan and grizzle; and look for the Them you can hate and the Us all ranged up against the Them. It was good being back in the factory. That's how it was good. I knew where I stood. Us, hammering away at all the Them, the bastards as grind you down.

I remember coming back one night from Oxford, and it was around four in the morning, and as we came in over the bridge to the Central station I could see the lights and the open door. Walking down the street from the station and in through the door, and the juke box was playing and there were two dancing couples, beautifully and slowly soft, and one behind the bar. There had been a good take-in from the till, and the coffee was still good and hot and fresh. There was blood on the floor, and the dirt from a fast night. It had a wonderful used look about it. It was an oasis in a city of the dead. The only place open. That was the way I liked it. That was the way it could have been. It became that night, both open and exclusive; the sort of place where I could feel proud at being a customer.

Evan, you once said to me that all I was was a bourgeois pig, doing good, running a social service for a people I looked down on.

No, that wasn't the trouble. It was the reverse. You see, for those and those like me who have come one remove from the old working class and been brought up in Bushland Road, and have found and hated the phoneyness, the niceness, the deadening effect of those psuedo middle-class roads with their nice decent dead outward faces, there is a wanting to move back with an aggressiveness, a passion, an all-consuming hatred, wanting to shout and scream all the way through till they reach the point where they know their own position, where they find their own place, their own life, life itself, and then and only then is it quiet. Only then when they have cleared themselves of all they didn't ask to be brought up with, only then can they start and look straight and begin to build. My time came in the middle of Leicester. That's the pity. That was the trouble. For while you're moving and clearing the rubble you can't stop yourself throwing mud back at where you came from, at The School, and the Bushland Roads.

Once I spent a whole night with Dave talking through what we were after, this central agency business. And one of the things that kept coming up again and again was getting on. Right so you come from the streets off Sparkenhoe, you come from the old working classes, and most of you go into the factory, into the ordinary job and earn just enough for the telly and a small car, and that's it. That's as far as it goes.

Now one of you starts up a little business, works his way up, educates himself, saves a little money, moves away from the old streets into some new estate. He gets a job where he isn't tied down like he was at the factory, and so on. Now we all want to get on. But most of us can't forget the old patterns.

But does this getting on have to mean a going out and away? Does it always have to mean a move into a middle class? Aren't we all aristocrats, aren't we all as our human right members of the one privileged class? It's just that some of us haven't the trimmings, or even the essentials that go with being an aristocrat in fact.

No, let's go back. You let us down, and you let us down badly. You and your words, and your writing more than anything. You let us down, let all us ordinary people who thought you'd do something; you let us down. You went off looking for the dirty side. With your flair for the seamy side you went on and on, and forgot us ordinary people who wanted something decent. We got our pride, and our dignity and you dragged it through the mud. Why? Why did you let us down? Why did you drag up the muck?

No, look, that was the last thing I wanted to see happen, the very last. But what I was batting against, was this idea of getting on; that to get on you have to stop being earthy, stop being yourself, and go all nice and decent and quiet and dead; that getting on didn't mean a car and a telly and a new house and a big garden and big money, but it meant a change in a way of life, a cultural movement from something that was good and wonderful and living to something that was a shell of a life. That was what I was frightened of, not that the thing might get a bad name, but that it might get pushed up into a good name and you know what I mean by good here, good and nice and lifeless and superficial and dead.

The greatness and wonder about the whole Leicester thing was that it didn't go that way. The tragedy was that it got taken, forced, pushed the other way. It was in the situation.

But what I saw, what I saw take place, the way it worked I never forget this.

I saw a pride and a power and a freedom. I saw a people rise up for a way of life, to claim their right. I saw something happen. I saw in fact what I'd only been able to dream about. It won't die. Things like that, they don't die. After the peace and after the sensation the workers move in, quietly behind the headlines and the work gets done, work I couldn't do. All I could dream of was a result, and I saw it start. It won't die. It'll come through again. It has to. It will do.

Nice and nasty, nice and naughty — and I sided with the nasty and the naughty, painting a seedy picture of tin pot skiffle groups, grubby lads and louts, a club no decent person would want to belong to, romancing on the seamy side — that what you meant, Rog, when you said I let down all you ordinary people, that I threw dirt in your faces. That what you meant, Johnny, when you said that I tagged on with Jim's band just because they were more on the Town than yours? That what you meant, Bill, when you stormed up to me with your why, why, why did I write the pamphlet? That what you meant, our Jim, when you kept on at me.

What was at the back of my mind?

Well, I tell you, right at the back, right at the back! We got a right to a car, and a big house and good food and our own music — what we need we have a right to, a right to as human beings.

But do we have, to get these things; do we have to squirm around in the real dirt, in the real seamy side, giving up a way of life that lives, something with dignity, an earthiness that breathes, a passion, a spontaneity, an immediacy of response;

do we have to give up all that and go mealy mouthed and sweet and nice and pigeon shitting, all gutless and like a shell of a man; do we have to go like that before we get anything?

Well, I tell you, I think we do, because that's the way it is. You fall in, and they turn you into shells, a shell of a man, deaden you into something worse than nothing; turn life into a charade, a make believe, a set of nice twee, twee manners.

That's what so good about jazz, about the teenage thing, about the club we nearly brought off. That's what was good about it. That it lives, and is honest and truthful and decent before that word got associated with a semi-detached house; decent in the human sense. And why didn't we bring it off?

Because as soon as you cut across, as soon as you say that you stand by the living, the honest, the true to life; by tin pot skiffle groups that are tin pot only because of a lack of money. As soon as you say that you stand by this, by a life and a warmth; as soon as you refuse to be pushed into a decency that has no meaning and is as empty as the shell it stands for; as soon as you do this you are turned on. It wasn't I who said we ran a club for sinners. I said we ran a club for our own and our own way of life. And the living, the truly decent, the honest, have only two ways, only two choices in the way things are — to go sweet smiles and hand in mouth, or to go their own way cutting across centuries of tradition and have the labels thrown on them — sexy, sinning, and not at all nice.

No, what I was scared of, was going nice, scared of getting pushed into a shell of the right and the dead and the semi-detached and all the things I'd fought against happening to me in Bushland Road and at The School, and The University; and so, well, I was going to move the other way. And not down, that was the last thing I wanted, and the first thing I got. No, don't drag it down. And don't push it up. It's so wonderful, so good as it is. Move it across, break through, make it richer, break open, cut across. But when you don't move up, they push you down.

That was the pity of the thing. That Leicester, that place and that people, the most wonderful people I had ever met, and it all got dragged down.

But what of me, what is it that has driven me on, through Leicester and after and out up again? Where do I go from here? Ah, I have tricks, I have things in my pockets, on the soles of my feet, and it's alright now. Leicester, I thank you. Never forget that city. Never forget those times. Never forget that people. Too good. Too sweet. Never forget.

thirteen

I WAS IN PARIS IN '58. JUST BEFORE DE GAULLE came in. I remember getting in a Peugot 403 outside an off Champs Elysees' club, and as we were crossing the Place de Concorde we hit broadside with this Citroen 2CV, and we all got out and everyone talked and tore away at each other, and then got back into the cars before the police came. I felt all alone, being the only one there who couldn't rattle off in French. Normally my little French will get me by, with my own English, wherever I go, but something like that happens and all of a sudden I know it's not enough, this moving around isn't enough. And when, like then, I was tired and a little tipsy, and being the only Englishman for miles around, and you've had a car smash, and you want desperately to talk your own kind of English to one of your own kind, and you start singing the *Northern Lights of Old Aberdeen*, or *Mad Dogs and Englishmen*, or *Ban the Bomb*, or something quite irrelevant and ridiculous, just to hear your own voice coming out in a language you know how to use. I remember that night, and after the car smash we went down to this little club in a cellar and they were playing Volare on the juke box. It was on the other side of the Seine. Funny thing, everywhere I went across Europe then they were playing Volare; and the room was full of smoke and suddenly across the French and the German came this English voice, as clear as a bell — Hey, Ray, you cheeky bastard — this tall blonde in a green thing. Last time I saw her was in the dive bar at Manchester. Recognised. Known. Just that. I was at home again. In my own country and it didn't matter that it was Paris or Rotterdam or Liverpool or London, or where the hell it was, or if it was an old friend or someone you met only two weeks ago and never seen since. That didn't matter. It was well gone four in the morning and I was in this cellar dive place off the left bank of the Seine in the middle of France, and it didn't matter.

I couldn't think of the blonde's name, but it didn't matter. I wasn't alone any more.

I've always wanted that — to be recognised. You've been away from this town for over two years, and then you're back and you're down and everyone knows you're down, and ever so slowly people start to nod, to wink, to speak, say how do. They ring at the front door. You haven't told anybody. You haven't written. And no one says how nice to see you again, or what have you been doing, or what are you going to do. They just nod — recognition, nothing more, nothing more at all. You matter. You're a part of other people's scenery, and not just a fact in a statistical report. You're not just a man who did this and that. You're a face, a person and you're not alone. It's all worthwhile.

You see at school I always felt out — out in the cold, torn between those who didn't want to take the 11-plus and wanted to get out and get a job; and those who wanted a degree and to be a better person and all that Sunday newspaper stuff. I felt terribly out all through school, and even more so at University. I went to find out, find out myself, my capabilities, my limitations, my likes and my place; and the green forgery proof piece of paper that would have come on with a successful end, it didn't mean a thing, didn't mean anything more than a toilet roll, not even that. It didn't even have that much use.

You wanted recognition, as a writer? As an intellectual? As a somebody? As something special apart?

No. No.

Are you sure?

Yes, I am sure, quite sure. I wanted recognition as a face, as flesh and blood and potential and past and future and present and mind and body. And simple recognition, of me as a person now with a history and qualities and those qualities as facts, and not as making me either better or superior or ordinary or a little too ordinary or any of the other little slots they try to put you in.

Are you sure it wasn't fame? Are you sure you haven't wanted to hear your name talked about on the tops of buses, to see your name in print, to be famous or notorious?

Maybe, yes, maybe but you see ...

Are you sure that it hasn't been fame that has driven you through these formative years, or whatever you want to call them? A little nobody at school so you had to do something wrong, or dramatic or startling to attract attention; perhaps even convince yourself that you were alive. Talking of leaving or resigning from every job you've ever had, to test and keep on testing where your popularity rating stood, to keep your name in the limelight. At respectable parties you have said and shocked — and this season when you want your party to go off with a bang invite that Mister G. and be amused. Invite and hear those working-class teddy boy words and see those working-class teddy boy winkle-pickers, and see those teddy boy manners — invite and give your guests that superior, I am so glad I am so above all of that, that omniscient feeling, we are so in contact with ordinary people. We see all sides of life. We know now. We have seen the genuine thing.

No, look you here — I am not the genuine thing. I have never met the genuine thing. I am me — m.e. — If I have shouted and screamed and if I am shouting and screaming away now and if I am shouting and screaming into the future it is because what I see around me, and what I hear you say, it grieves me — look can't you see. And now it's under control.

You stand on the lecture platform and you get introduced and they always say the wrong things about you, and you blush and go a little red in the face, and you stand up with a few notes and a few lines of argument in your hand, light a cigarette and take a gulp at the glass of water and hope you haven't taken too much so you might have to go out for a piss before you finished what you have to say. You look at the faces round the room. You smile and cough, and open your mouth and hope, speak. Words are wonderful and English it's so wonderful, such a wonderful language — accents, intonations, pauses — like an actor — my script, my notes, a point to get across and a hundred ways of doing it — and I can alter the way of coming to you — the form of words, the method and watch the faces — you bored, all you at the back, right let me try it this way; try this way, it might work now it sounds superficial, too earthy, well, it's meant to be but look, let me try it another way, put in another set of references, then there's another chance for you, and as importantly, for me to see why — change, chop, flow to the faces out there, and to the way your own echo comes back at you — it's good, wonderful, every minute of it.

But there's a temptation. Half way through I want to stop and close the notes and light another cigarette and smile down and look man, look I'm working for your attention every moment. But what right have I got to stand up here and talk to you. I'm in a mess. It's like a skyscraper that gets quarter of the way up when they decide they didn't want it on that site after all, and so they pull it all down. I'm up to my ears in it. What right have I? You're older than I am, and you don't drink in the same sort of bars. You have time to think. You have time to go to lectures like this one. Perhaps you can tell me what to do with Me. Look, I want you to give me a talk.

But I never do. I carry on, right to the end, and then tea, and the trip back.

Where you bin, our Ray?

Bin giving a lecture.

Cheeky bastard, how you do it?

Alright. I get through. It's worth it.

What you talk about?

You and me and them and things.

Did you put your act on?

For a little.

But I like it best in pubs, like cabaret. You start off sitting on the edge listening to the talk and then you move in without any introductions, right in, getting all worked up to a climax, and the crowd round you, they move along with you, till you're all talking in a hot language and people are laughing, proper laughs. When I talk to students they take me seriously, and the wrong things seriously, and they listen. They're never with me, or showing they're against me. In pubs and at the factory they laugh and respond, not because they think it's funny, but because they know it's true, and you take it with a pinch of salt because you know if you weren't a laughing you'd be a roaring. It's better that way.

Ah, you're so unstable.

You're so dead right. I move with the wind; well, you know what, let the wind blow round me and feel it blowing. And lectures and tub thumpings and things like that, they ought to be camp and funny and anecdotal and dramatic and personal. I should have the guts and the verve to carry through to the end, and not stop half way through to wonder where I'm going. When you're asked to give a talk. When you're paid. When someone says what do you think, and you're paid to do this to a group of people who of their own free will have come to hear you, and you're recognised and you have a public face and all that; you've got to keep up to it. Be funny and personal and shocking. Give them just what they expect and something new, the next stage on. You have a duty to hold them, to grip their attention. I am not required to be educated or learned. I am supposed to have a ground-level contact. I am supposed to know ground level and be earthy. That's why I am here. That's why they have come. They have paid their money to join this society, and they have given up so many hours of their time to make the journey to hear you. Remember that — yes — yes — I do. I do indeed. But I can't help feeling that ... You see, there is a conflict. I want them to give me something, but it can't be that way. I am paid to give.

They are the ones who have paid to take.

Is it fame?

Yes, in a way I love it. And I'll go when they invite me, as long as they pay me.

You love yourself don't you? You love to stand up there on some high horse and preach and use the power of words and movement and watch their faces light up and shine and call out your name and be talked about?

Yes, yes, alright, alright, and also the anti-climax when they don't quite get what they expected. And also that wonderful feeling, so wonderful that you know you have got across to other people what you know, have thought, have felt. Yes, I love it.

You too have wanted to be a pop star?

It's a thought. To stand up there, curtains drawn across and you put out your left hand and point. They scream and the drums roll, and the guitar plucks and you're away up there on your high horse in a blue spot. You walk right into the spot. You raise a leg, move over, cross over, move out to meet the spot again and let the light fall full on your face. You grip the microphone. It's the instrument, the method; like the spot the thing you have to walk into and control; your public image and you love it more than anything. It's your agent and your affair and your mother and your god—screams, shouts, people running. There's a crowd in front. You smile, open your mouth and wriggle. They scream your name. Your public image made up from your private parts, be it soul or skin or mind. That doesn't matter. They all crowd around you and say such a remarkable young man, and you smile and take a bottle of beer from a stage-hand and pour the beer all over the head and uplifted face of the one nearest to you; symbolic. The stupid little bastards. The great big phoneys.

Alright. You win. So you pour beer over their faces and show that you don't care a damn, but you love yourself, don't you?

Yes, I do. The microphone in front of you. The walkie talkie creepy crawly. The wire mesh or the double-barrelled eye. An improvised studio, full of smoke, BBC on the front, or K25, or RTF. A woman's voice, like an interpreter. You reply. Flicking ash across the microphone. There's a play back. You can hear it — flick, flick, flick — as the ash fell from your cigarette as you tapped it across the microphone. No good. Start again. The play back you can't hear. And then on the day you forget to listen, and people tell you — you were alright but... I don't care. I don't care. Being alright, it isn't good enough. It won't do. You're either good or you're no good. Fame, it makes no difference. Don't you believe it. I have only wetted my lips with all this, but the taste was good. Not in itself, but because through this you can say what you want to say, and you get paid for it, so you have time to really work on how you want to get across what you have to say. And also I've stopped being afraid. I write something down. I know it's not how it could be, but I send it off with no corrections, no comments and wait for the reply; and then when the reply arrives I work from there, or if the comment comes back and it's no good then I read the piece through and if I think the comment's fair, then I leave it — no take off there. Try another way. And then send it out and back, and so on till I get it just how I want it, or the nearest I think I can possibly get.

Yes, yes. I want the spot to hug me. I want to hold that microphone in my hand. I want all this. But I don't want to force myself on to these screens and screeds.* And more than that, I'm not going to be forced. If the fans want you I'll play the tune and do the party piece and then when they're all there I'll do my own little bit. If they don't. If they won't. If they can't take this, then I'll go back. Back to the factory and the five to seven bus into the centre. You see, it doesn't matter whether it's Oxford, or a pub in the Midlands or the factory bench I am bound, I cannot help but get up on my little stool and scream away, sound the trumpets and thump. The joy and the lurve is just as great in the public bar as it is in the student hall. The one trouble is that in the public bar it is limited. The effect is smaller, however deeper it goes it misses the width.

Don't you see, what I see around me, it moves me so much. I can't keep it in.

.   .   .

When I was sixteen or so, I saw a film called *Giant* — story — young half-caste Texan owns a little square of land in a big white man's estate. Big white man in cattle and worth millions. Half-caste does smallholding to keep himself alive in the essentials, and then digs down for oil. Oil comes to Texas. The half-caste finds it first and gets richer and bigger and faster than the big white man. He gets as rich as the big white man. The struggle is over. Big rich half-caste, now aged

---

*   Script-writing.

sixtyish—degenerate, rich and big and nasty as big white man. Big celebration after the war. Jettexas, the half-caste, lays on great celebration, and invites the big white man. Big white man has a fight with the half-caste. Half-caste loses. Too degenerate, bad blood. Then half-caste has to make a speech. Falls down in the middle of the speech. Knocked out with all the years of struggle. Everyone follows big white man. Back where we are. Moral — half-caste may find oil but doesn't know what to do with it. Big white man does. Big white men always win.

From fifteen, sixteen I fought on my little plot of land. I fought for the ideas, for a warmth I saw slowly getting bogged up by The School, by all the big and little white men who supported the big white man. I fought for my own, and at twenty I came through with all the cards in my hand. I made a mess of it. I had my fight with the big white man, and the big white man, he won, and it was my fault and not his that I lost. I made the speech, and I was left with the ruins. But I'm lucky. I did it all in two years. And now I'm left, and have been down and now up again, with enough gut and verve to start all over again.

I came in with James Dean, crawling on the roadway shouting and weeping and all very aggressive about poor little me; they're all messing it up. But just you wait till the oil comes to my plot of land. I'll show you. And the oil came, and I bullsed it up, good and proper. And now I start again, and it isn't like that any more.

The teddy suit has gone, and given way to the Italian thing. The aggression has moved into an arrogance. This hip, this reaction from an all-pervading niceness, it's got in place. The dignity has come back, and the anarchy and aggression, the tin pot, seedy, grubby and screaming selections have gone, and the vision is that much clearer. The fight against all them has moved into an arrogance, this sure knowledge that we're going to come through, oil or no oil. We're going through the rubble and tin cans and we're picking out the ones that will be of use, and clearing the site and digging the foundations, and then build, build. And you, the brain behind the dark glasses at Blackpool, you have no relevance. You may try to do your best to do good for The People but it doesn't mean a thing. You're on the other side. And we'll work on, under the Edwardian myth, building and building and going on independently of all your shy pride and past glories and subtle niceties. You see, I don't have to shout at you now. I'm certain. Positive. I stay on the ground. I've cleared the site, and I'm making the foundations and I've still got the jerries laid on in case I strike oil. Waiting for that click, again; for the oil and when it comes, if it comes, I know I'll have the pipelines and jerries all laid on, and they will be alright, and more than alright and they'll work, and the oil will turn out into a freedom and a cash. Oh, now look, I haven't bought this plot of land. I was born with it. It's my birthright, and on it is still this smallholding that keeps me in essentials, the necessities — that is my right, as a human being. I didn't have to ask for it. I didn't have to assert it. It's a fundamental. But the oil is the dream, the milk and honey on the other side. I haven't given that up, but it's a dream; a dream than can come true. It came true once and it can come true again. But in the meantime there's no use being aggressive and screaming at all the big white men who still own, possess the big estates, like they possess their women. No, I am building on my plot of land, building in spite of and by making use of the things, the rubble and tin cans left over, and stolen and thrown away from the big white man's place. Build, build in arrogance and pride and warmth and colour and all the primary things we almost lost, that almost got taken over.

And all the time I wander round this plot of land, and I still keep the dream. I polish and clean the jerries and pipelines so that if it comes I won't miss it. If it doesn't I still make the most of what I've got. After all it's the only one I know I shall ever have. Don't mess it around. And don't kill the dream.

We all move on, all of us, and You who started all this—remember—Manchester and you looked up at me and you said you had come a hundred miles—no—even if it were 500—makes no difference—we all move on, all of us. You, you should have taken your chances, made the most of it—always make the most of it, never let go, it might be the only one, ever. I looked all rich and well in Manchester. Not like when you knew me down Leicester, all tatty and tired. You should have taken your chances then. Now it's too late. I'm in another city. And it's wonderful. It might be the last. It might be the only one. Any road, I'm not letting go. Make the most of it. I'm not letting go, not never.

POMONA BOOKS

POMONA IS A WHOLLY INDEPENDENT PUBLISHER DEDICATED to bringing before the public the work of prodigiously talented writers. Tell your friends. Our books can be purchased on-line at:

www.pomonauk.com

Also available:

FOOTNOTE *
by Boff Whalley

ISBN 1-904590-00-4

£8.99

FOOTNOTE IS CLEVER, FUNNY AND IRREVERENT — A STORY ABOUT A boy from the redbrick clichés of smalltown England reconciling Mormonism and punk rock, industrial courtesy and political insurrection.

He finds a guitar, anarchism and art terrorism and, after years (and years and years) of earnest, determined, honest-to-goodness slogging, his pop group† makes it big; that's BIG with a megaphone actually. They write a song that has the whole world singing and, funnily enough, it's an admirable summary of a life well lived — about getting knocked down and getting back up again.

Meanwhile, there's a whole world still happening: authentic lives carefully drawn, emotional but not sentimental and always with a writer's eye for detail. *Footnote* is not another plodding rock memoir but a compassionate, critical and sometimes cynical account of a life steeped in pop culture, lower division football and putting the world to rights.

---

* See page 293 of Boff Whalley's book.

† Boff Whalley is a member of Chumbawamba.

RULE OF NIGHT
by Trevor Hoyle

ISBN 1-904590-01-2

£8.99

IF THE SIXTIES WERE SWINGING, THE SEVENTIES WERE THE HANG-
over — darker, nastier, uglier — especially if you lived on a council estate in
the north of England.

Rule of Night was first published in 1975 and has since become a cult
classic. It pre-dates the current vogue for 'hard men' and 'football hoolie'
books by 25 years.

It is, however, much more than this. Trevor Hoyle creates a chillingly
detailed world, where teenagers prowl rainy fluorescent-lit streets dressed
as their *Clockwork Orange* anti-heroes. The backdrop is provided by Ford
Cortinas, Players No.6, the factory, the relentless struggle to maintain hope.

Hoyle, who has since been published by John Calder (home to Samuel
Beckett and William S. Burroughs), has added a fascinating afterword to
his original book which has been out of print and highly sought-after for
many years.

THE FAN
by Hunter Davies

ISBN 1-904590-02-0

£9.99

HUNTER DAVIES IS ONE OF BRITAIN'S MOST ACCLAIMED WRITERS and journalists. He has written over 30 books, among them modern classics, *The Beatles* and *A Walk Around The Lakes*. *The Glory Game*, published in 1972, is a benchmark work on football and is still in print today.

The Fan is a collection of very personal, unusual pieces about his life as a supporter. He observes football in its sovereignty of the late 1900s and early 2000s and tackles the big topics of the day: Beckham's haircuts, high finance, the price of pies, the size of match day programmes, the enormous wages, the influence of Sky TV, England's numerous managers.

Along the way, he also lets us into his home life, in London and the Lake District, his family, his work, his tortoise, his poorly knee (caused by too much Sunday football).

Originally published in the *New Statesman* magazine, *The Fan* catches Davies at his very best and most amusing. It will appeal to supporters of any age, sex and loyalties.

LOVE   SONGS
by Crass

ISBN 1-904590-03-9

£9.99

Our love of life is total,
everything we do is an expression of that.
Everything that we write is a love song.
– Penny Rimbaud, *Yes, Sir, I Will*

CRASS: A RURAL COLLECTIVE BASED IN ESSEX, FORMED IN 1977 OF A
diverse and eclectic group of individuals who operated for several years
using music, art, literature and film as vehicles to share information and
ideas. They also wanted to change the world.

This is a collection of words spanning those seven short years; a book of
shock slogans and mindless token tantrums. An anthology of passionate
love songs that sought to inspire a generation, and succeeded.

FORTHCOMING TITLES

more details: www.pomonauk.com

POMONA SOUNDS

POMONA SOUNDS IS OUR AFFILIATED RECORD LABEL.
The following CD albums are available on-line at :

www.pomonauk.com:

PS-001	The Rosenbergs *Ameripop*	£7
PS-002	Black September *Black September*	£10
PS-003	Mudskipper *Eggshells*	£10
PS-004	The Monkey Run *Escape From The Rake*	£10
PS-005	Crass *You'll Ruin It For Everyone*	£10
PS-006	Killing Stars *When The Light First Fell*	£10
PS-007	Black September *You Can Do Anything If You Set Your Mind To It*	£10

THERE'S

TO

THAN

KNOW,

BUT

NOT MUCH MORE.